# Women Too Tired to Keep Pretending

A Practical Guide for the Overwhelmed to Reduce Stress, Lighten the Invisible Load, Stop People-Pleasing, and Reclaim Who You Were

## George Munson

GL DIGITAL PUBLISHING LLC

# Contents

# Introduction

## You Are Not Failing. You Are Depleted.

The journey begins ...

The car was still moving when the realization hit. It wasn't moving fast, maybe five miles per hour, but it was drifting backward down the driveway while the driver's side door swung wide open.

Sarah Miller had one foot on the pavement and one hand gripping the steering wheel, her body twisted in a panicked, awkward stretch. She had jumped out because she realized, with a jolt of pure electricity in her chest, that her three-year-old's favorite stuffed rabbit was still sitting on the kitchen island. Without that rabbit, preschool drop-off would be a scene of emotional devastation. Without that rabbit, her carefully timed morning would collapse, making her late for the 9:00 a.m. project sync, which would make her late for the 2:00 p.m. budget review, which would mean she'd be answering emails at midnight.

The hidden mental load that women often carry can lead to moments of stress and distraction, such as forgetting to put the car in park or feeling unsteady on their feet. For a second, time slowed down. She saw the neighbor's mailbox getting closer. She felt the SUV's heavy weight pulling away from her. With a desperate lunging kick, she slammed her right foot onto the brake pedal. Commuting is considered one of life's least enjoyable experiences and is closely linked to increased stress levels. She sat motionless for a long minute, her forehead pressed to the cold leather of the steering wheel, as the car jerked to a stop and the tires chirped. Her heart was drumming against her ribs like a trapped bird. She wasn't hurt. The car was fine. The rabbit was still on the counter. But as she sat in the silence of her driveway, Sarah didn't feel relieved. She felt like she was breaking.

The car was only part of it. Her brain had become so crowded with school theme days, grocery lists, aging parents' doctor appointments, and work deadlines that there was no room left for basic physics. She was a high-achieving woman, a project manager who could handle million-dollar budgets, yet she was currently losing a fight with a driveway and a stuffed bunny.

If you are reading this, you probably know that feeling. It is the feeling of being "on" but never "present." It is the sensation of your jaw clenching at 2:00 p.m. for no reason you can name, or the way your stomach drops when you hear a notification chime on your phone. You aren't just tired; you are depleted.

## The Quiet Crisis of the "Fine" Woman

There is a specific kind of exhaustion that sleep cannot fix. It is the weight of being the "Human Sticky Note" for everyone in your life. You are the one who remembers that it's library book day. You are the one who notices the milk is low. According to Psychology Today, women often take on the responsibility of managing the emotional climate at work and at home, usually without acknowledgment. For years, women have also been described as natural multitaskers. We have been sold the idea that we are built for this, that our brains are wired to juggle twelve flaming torches while smiling for a holiday card photo. But the truth is much darker. We aren't natural multitaskers; we are just chronically over-extended.

When you live in this state for too long, your body starts to change. When you stay in survival mode, your mind shifts to focus entirely on detecting threats and protecting yourself, making it even harder to manage additional demands from others. You start to feel like a ghost in your own life, watching yourself move through the motions of making school lunches and attending Zoom calls, while the "real you" is buried somewhere under a mountain of laundry and unread texts.

This isn't a personal flaw. You haven't failed at "having it all." You are a highly functional person living in a low-functioning system. Our modern world was built on the assumption that someone, usually a woman, would be home to handle the invisible details. Now, we are doing the work, the home, the caregiving, and the mental management of it all, and we are doing it without the "village" we were promised.

## What This Book Is Not

Most books for tired women are just more items for your to-do list. They tell you to wake up at 5:00 a.m. to meditate, start a complicated gratitude journal, or "optimize" your meal prep.

If you are currently so tired that you sometimes forget your own middle name, the last thing you need is a "productivity hack." You don't need to be more efficient at being exhausted. You don't need a pastel-colored planner or a lecture on "mindset."

This book is a way out of the fog. It is a guide to understanding the biology of your stress so you can stop blaming yourself for it. By the time you reach the final page, you won't just have a cleaner kitchen or a better calendar. You will finally have *yourself* back.

You will learn:

- Why your brain feels "fried" and how to reset your nervous system in less than a minute.

- How to name the "invisible labor" you do so you can finally stop carrying it all alone.

- Why "self-care" as we know it is a lie, and what actually works to bring you back to life.

- How to set boundaries that don't leave you with a "guilt hangover."

- The art of being "enough" in a world that demands perfection.

## Why You Can Trust This Path

I didn't write this from a mountaintop of perfect peace. I wrote this from the trenches. I have lived the 2:00 a.m. spiral where you stare at the ceiling and wonder why you feel so angry at people you love. I have stood in the grocery store aisle and cried because they were out of the specific brand of yogurt your kid eats, and you realized you didn't have the "mental energy" to make a new choice.

But I also spent years talking to psychologists, and women who felt the same way. What I found was a pattern. The women who found their way back to calm didn't do it by working harder. They did it by understanding how their bodies process stress and by lowering the bar until it hit the floor.

The science is clear: your brain is not betraying you. It is trying to protect you. When you feel "on edge," your nervous system is doing its job. It just doesn't realize that a missed deadline isn't a saber-toothed tiger. It is possible to help individuals regain a sense of emotional safety.

## Meet Sarah

Throughout this book, we will follow Sarah Miller (a fictional character). Sarah is 39 years old and lives in a suburb of Columbus, Ohio. She's a project manager, a wife to Mark, and a mother to two kids who seem to grow out of their shoes every three weeks. She is witty, kind, and incredibly good at her job.

To the outside world, Sarah is "killing it." Her kids are clean, her work projects are on time, and she always remembers her mother-in-law's birthday. But inside, Sarah feels like a computer with too many tabs open.

She is "The Human Sticky Note." She holds the entire structure of her family's life in her head until her scalp literally hurts.

When we meet her in these pages, Sarah is at a breaking point. She's tired of being the only one who notices when the toilet paper runs out. She's tired of the "mental load" that makes her feel like a manager instead of a person. She wants to remember who she was before her life became a series of logistical puzzles to solve.

Sarah's story is the story of so many of us. As we walk through the tools in this book, we will watch Sarah try them out. We'll see her fail, we'll see her struggle with the guilt of saying "no," and eventually, we'll see her breathe again.

## The Journey Ahead

We are going to start by looking at those "spinning plates" you're holding and why it's okay to let a few of them smash on the floor. We'll look at the science of your "survival mode" so you can stop wondering why you're so snappy. We will tackle the invisible work that no one sees, but everyone relies on.

Most importantly, we are going to talk about the woman you used to be, the one who had hobbies, who laughed until she cried, and who didn't spend her 2:00 a.m. hours worrying about soccer practice. She is still in there. She's just buried under a lot of noise.

This book is meant to be read in the quiet moments, in the car while you wait for practice to end, in the ten minutes before bed, or in the bathroom where no one can find you. You don't have to read it perfectly. You don't have to do every exercise. You have to show up.

The life you are living right now is loud, fast, and heavy. But there is a version of your life that feels quiet, steady, and light. It isn't a fairy tale, and it doesn't require you to move to a deserted island. It just requires a different way of being in the world you already have.

Take a deep breath. Let your shoulders drop half an inch. You aren't failing. You are just depleted. And it's time to come back.

Let's begin.

---

# Chapter One

# The Spinning Plates

## And Why One Always Seems Ready to Fall

On Tuesday, October 12th, Sarah Miller woke up at 6:14 a.m., exactly sixty seconds before her alarm was set to go off. For a moment, she lay in the gray morning light, listening to the hum of the refrigerator downstairs and the soft, rhythmic breathing of her husband, Mark. This was her favorite minute of the day. It was the only time she wasn't being asked for a snack, a signature, or a status update.

By 6:15 a.m., the silence was shattered. The phone on her nightstand buzzed with a notification from the school PTA app. A volunteer had backed out of the fall festival. Then a text from her boss: *The client wants the deck by noon, not EOD. Can we make it happen?*

Sarah swung her feet onto the floor. Her day didn't start with a slow rise; it started with a sprint. She moved through the kitchen like a dealer at a high-stakes poker table, sliding bread into the toaster while checking the weather on her tablet. She realized it was "Wacky Wednesday" for her youngest child, which meant she had to find a pair of mismatched socks and some hair glitter in the next twenty minutes.

As she poured the coffee, she was already mentally calculating the shelf life of the milk, the probability of her car hitting empty before she reached the office, and whether she had remembered to RSVP to her sister's baby shower. These micro-plates often go unnoticed but contribute to the constant mental effort many women experience daily.

She felt proud of this skill. Society told her it was her superpower. "I don't know how you do it all!" her neighbor would say with a mix of awe and pity. Sarah would smile and shrug, even though the truth was that her brain felt like a browser window with sixty-five tabs open, all of them playing a different song at the same time.

## The Invisible Architecture

We often think of our "to-do list" as a physical thing, like a piece of paper or an app where we check off tasks. But the real weight of a woman's life is the **cognitive overhead-those invisible plates-that vary for each person. Recognizing your unique mental load is the first step to managing it effectively**. This is the invisible architecture of your day. It is the mental energy required to keep track of everything that needs to be done.

Imagine every task you have is a physical plate. Most of us think we are only spinning three or four big ones: Work, Parenting, Marriage, and Home. But if you look closer, each of those big plates is actually made up of dozens of tiny, vibrating saucers. To manage your mental load, try listing these plates and then prioritizing them based on urgency and importance. This helps you see where your energy is truly needed and where you can delegate or pause.

Take "Parenting." It isn't one plate. It is a stack of twenty. There is the "School Communication" plate, which requires you to read three emails a day and remember which kid needs a permission slip for the zoo. There is the "Growth Tracking" plate, where you notice that the sleeves on your son's coat are suddenly two inches too short. There is the "Social Management" plate, where you coordinate playdates so your children don't become outcasts.

When Sarah was standing in her kitchen that Tuesday, she wasn't simply making toast. She was managing the **Labor of Noticing, an ongoing mental process that many women feel guilty about not acknowledging. Recognizing that this labor is constant can help you accept that prioritizing some plates over others is necessary for your well-being. It's okay to focus on what truly matters and temporarily let go of less urgent tasks**.

This labor has no "off" switch. It runs in the background of your brain like a computer program that never closes, slowly draining your battery until you find yourself staring at a grocery store shelf, unable to remember whether you actually need eggs or if you just dreamt you did. Knowing this can help women feel understood and less alone in their mental load.

## The Myth of the Natural Multitasker

For decades, we have been told a very specific lie: Women are better at multitasking than men. We've heard it in jokes, seen it in commercials for laundry detergent, and even read it in pop-psychology articles. It's sold as a biological gift, a secret weapon that allows us to be the CEO and the Room Mom at the same time.

But the science tells a different story. Human beings, regardless of gender, cannot actually multitask. Our brains are not designed to process two complex streams of information at once. Recognizing this can help women feel more compassionate toward themselves and less pressured to do it all at once.

Every time that spotlight swings, there is a "switching cost." Your brain has to pause, reorient, and load the rules for the new task. If you are writing a work email and your child asks you where their library book is, your brain has to drop the professional language, load the "home map" of the living room, solve the problem, and then try to find its way back to that email.

Studies show that this constant switching can lower your functional IQ by ten points. This leads to a state of "continuous partial attention," in which you are never fully present in any given moment because you are always preparing for the next switch.

The reason women *seem* better at it isn't that our brains are different; it's because we have been socialized to accept the interruption. We have been trained to believe that being "available" is part of our job description. We don't multitask because we're gifted; we multitask because we're drowning, and we're trying to keep every plate from shattering at once.

## The Failing vs. Excelling Paradox

There is a strange phenomenon that happens to high-achieving women. The better you are at spinning plates, the more "failing" you feel.

Sarah Miller is the perfect example. On paper, her Tuesday was a success. She turned in the deck by noon. She found the mismatched socks. She managed the dog's vet appointment over her lunch break. To anyone watching, she was excelling.

But when Sarah got into bed that night, she didn't feel like a winner. She felt like a fraud. She lay awake thinking about the five seconds she had snapped at her daughter for dropping a juice box. She worried that she hadn't been "engaged" enough during the client call because she was secretly checking the vet's portal for test results.

This is the **High-Achiever Paradox**. Because you are capable of doing so much, you raise the bar for yourself until it is physically impossible to reach. You stop measuring your success by what you *did* and start measuring it by how you *felt* while doing it. And because you felt frantic, distracted, and "on edge," you conclude that you must be failing.

We live in a culture that rewards the "hustle," but it doesn't provide the systems to support it. You are expected to work as if you don't have children or parents who don't have a job. When those two worlds collide, which they do every single day, the friction creates a heat that eventually leads to burnout.

## Anticipatory Labor, or the Energy of "What If"

One of the heaviest plates Sarah spins is one she doesn't even realize she's holding. It's called **Anticipatory Labor**. This is the energy used to prevent plates from dropping in the future.

It's the mental work of thinking, *If I don't defrost the chicken now, it won't be ready by 5:00 p.m., and if it's not ready by 5:00 p.m., we'll have to get takeout, which will make us late for soccer practice.*

It is a constant "chess game" played against a future version of yourself. You are trying to protect your future self from stress, but in doing so, you are exhausting your present self. You are solving problems that haven't happened yet.

This is why you feel so tired even when you are "relaxing." You might be sitting on the couch watching a movie, but half of your brain is calculating the logistics of tomorrow morning. You aren't resting; you are just in a "low-power mode" while your processors continue to churn through data.

This constant state of "scanning for threats," whether those threats are a missed deadline or a forgotten snack, keeps your body in a state of low-level alarm. You are waiting for the sound of a plate breaking. And when you live your life waiting for a crash, you can never truly be at peace.

## The Labor of Noticing

To understand why your plates feel so heavy, we have to look at who is doing the **noticing** in your life.

In most households, there is a "Manager" and a "Doer." The Doer might be happy to help. They'll fold the laundry if you ask, or pick up the milk if you put it on the list. But the Manager is the one who has to notice that the laundry basket is full and that the milk carton feels light.

The act of "noticing" is a full-time job. It requires a constant, total awareness of the environment. When you are the one noticing things in your family, you aren't just doing the work; you are responsible for the existence of the work.

Sarah realized this during a small moment on Saturday morning. Mark asked her, "Do we have any more lightbulbs?"

It was a simple question. But to Sarah, it felt like a heavy weight. To answer it, she had to stop what she was doing, mentally scan the utility closet, remember whether she had used the last one three weeks ago, and then decide whether to add it to the list.

"I don't know, Mark," she said, her voice tighter than she intended. "Can you just look?"

Mark was confused by her irritation. He was asking a question. But Sarah wasn't reacting to the question; she was reacting to the fact that she was the only one who held the "Lightbulb Status" in her brain. She was the one who kept the inventory of their entire life.

When you are the only one noticing, you are never off duty. Even when you are sleeping, your brain is "on call" for the next lightbulb, the next permission slip, or the next emotional crisis.

## Naming Your Plates

Before we can figure out how to stop the spinning, we have to see the plates for what they actually are. We often keep our stress in a vague, blurry cloud. We say, "I'm just overwhelmed," or "Life is crazy right now." But vagueness is the enemy of calm.

When we name the specific labor we are doing, we give it boundaries. We turn it from an invisible ghost into something real we can handle.

## The Plate Inventory Checklist

Look at these categories. Which of these are you currently holding? Don't just look at the big ones; look for the "micro-plates" hiding underneath.

- **Primary Earner/Professional Growth**: This includes doing the job, plus the energy of "staying relevant" and managing office politics.

- **Medical Tracker**: Knowing who needs a dentist appointment, whose vaccines are due, and which kid has a weird cough that needs watching.

- **The Social Secretary**: Managing the family calendar, buying birthday gifts for cousins, and responding to group texts.

- **The Emotional Thermostat**: Noticing when your partner is grumpy, when your child is anxious, or when your mother feels "left out."

- **The Aesthetic Manager**: Noticing when the house feels "cluttered," when the towels smell musty, or when the pillows need fluffing.

- **The Anticipator**: Planning for next season's clothes, next week's meals, and next year's vacation.

- **The Person Who Notices When Things Run Out**: Soap, toilet paper, ketchup, patience.

When Sarah looked at a list like this, she felt a strange mix of relief and anger. She was relieved to see that her exhaustion had a name. It wasn't that she was "weak"; she was carrying a list that would require a staff of five to handle well.

But she also felt a spark of anger. Why was she the only one who knew where the lightbulbs were? Why was she the one who felt the "guilt" when a plate dropped, even if it was a plate she never asked to carry in the first place?

## Name One Plate

You cannot drop all your plates today. If you tried, the chaos would likely create more stress than the spinning does. But you can begin the process of un-blurring your life.

Today, please pick one plate. It shouldn't be a big one like "My Career." Pick a microplate. Maybe it's "The Person Who Knows Where the Shoes Are" or "The Manager of the School App."

Don't try to change it yet. Don't try to delegate it. Don't even complain about it.

Just name it. Say it out loud or write it in the notes app on your phone. *"I am currently holding the plate of 'Remembering Everyone's Birthday.' This takes energy. This is real work."*

There is power in the naming. When you name a task, you validate the energy it takes to do it. You stop telling yourself that you're "doing nothing" and start acknowledging that you are, in fact, doing a great deal.

Sarah tried this. She picked the "Wacky Wednesday" plate. She realized that the stress of finding mismatched socks wasn't about the socks; it was the energy of *anticipating* her daughter's disappointment if she didn't have them. She named it. "I am holding the 'Parental Performance' plate."

As she said it, her shoulders dropped just a fraction of an inch. The plate didn't go away, but for the first time, she could see it. It was no longer part of her identity; it was just something she was holding.

## The Breaking Point

We have been taught that the goal of a "good woman" is to keep all the plates in the air forever. We treat a dropped plate as a moral failure. If the house is messy, we are "lazy." If we miss a deadline, we are "unprofessional." If our kids are unhappy, we are "bad mothers."

But here is the truth that Sarah Miller was starting to realize as she sat in her driveway that Tuesday morning: **Some plates are meant to break.**

Some of the things you are holding are not glass. They are plastic. If you drop the "Perfectly Curated School Lunch" plate, it won't shatter. It will just bounce. Your child will still eat. The world will still turn.

The problem is that when you are in survival mode, everything looks like glass. You treat the mismatched socks with the same level of urgency as the million-dollar budget. You treat the dust on the baseboards like a life-or-death emergency.

When your brain is constantly scanning for threats, it loses the ability to prioritize. Everything becomes a "Priority 1." This is why you feel so "fried." Your nervous system is screaming at you to save the socks, save the project, save the milk, and save the marriage all at the same time.

But you are not a machine. You have a finite amount of energy, and you are currently trying to power a city with a single AA battery.

## The Hope in the Chaos

If you are feeling the weight of your spinning plates right now, I want you to know that the feeling of "failing" is actually a sign of your intelligence. Your body is telling you that the system is broken. It is a signal, not a sentence.

You aren't failing at life; you're just trying to live an impossible version of it.

Sarah Miller didn't fix her life that Tuesday. She still had to go to work, and she still had to find that stuffed rabbit. But she did something different that night. When she got into bed, instead of running through the "Failure Reel" in her head, she thought about the "Naming" exercise.

She looked at her sleeping husband and realized that he wasn't "lazy"; he just wasn't "noticing." And he wasn't noticing because she had spent ten years making sure he never had to. She had been so good at spinning the plates that everyone else in her life had forgotten the plates even existed.

The path to calm doesn't start with doing more. It starts with seeing the invisible work and realizing that you have a choice. You can continue to spin until you collapse, or you can start to decide which plates are actually worth your precious, limited energy.

But before we can decide what to drop, we have to understand why it feels so physically painful to even think about letting go. We have to look at what is happening inside your brain when you feel that "snap" coming on.

Why does a spilled glass of water feel like a catastrophe? Why does a polite "no" feel like a threat to your safety? To answer that, we have to go deeper than your to-do list. We have to go into your biology.

The reason you can't "just relax" isn't because you're too busy. It's because your body doesn't think it's safe to stop. And until we teach your nervous system that the world won't end if a plate falls, you will always be one mismatched sock away from a breakdown.

# Chapter Two

# The Science of Survival Mode

## Your Brain Is Not Betraying You

If you saw Sarah Miller sitting in her parked car outside the grocery store on a Thursday afternoon, you would see a scene of suburban peace. The sun was hitting her windshield at just the right angle to make her hair look shiny and healthy. She was sipping a cold latte. From the outside, she looked like a woman who had her life completely under control, a project manager who had just finished a successful meeting, a mother who was ahead of schedule for the evening pick-up.

What you wouldn't see was that Sarah had been sitting there for twenty minutes, staring at a bag of frozen peas in her passenger seat, unable to move her arms. She wasn't crying. She wasn't even thinking about her to-do list. She was "gone." Her eyes were fixed on the store's logo, but her brain felt like a television set that had been unplugged mid-movie. The screen was black, and the room was silent.

This was the secret Sarah kept from everyone: she was "glitching."

Five minutes earlier, inside the store, a stranger had accidentally bumped her cart. It was a tiny thing. The woman had apologized and smiled. But for Sarah, that small bump felt like a physical assault. Her heart had surged into her throat. Her vision had blurred at the edges. She felt a sudden, hot wave of rage so intense she had to grip the handle of the cart to keep from screaming. She didn't scream, of course. She was a "good girl." She nodded, managed a tight smile, and walked as fast as she could to her car.

Now, she sat in the silence, her heart still thudding, her jaw locked so tight it hurt. She didn't understand why her body was reacting to a bump from a shopping cart as if it were a high-speed car chase. Recognizing these physical reactions as signs of stress can help women like Sarah become more aware of their nervous system's signals, so they can take steps to manage their reactions before they escalate.

But the truth is exactly the opposite. Sarah's brain isn't broken. It's working perfectly to help her survive, which can help women feel more understanding and less self-critical about their stress responses.

## The Ghost of the Savannah

To understand why Sarah felt as if she were dying in a grocery store parking lot, we have to travel back several hundred thousand years. We have to look at the "Origin Story" of the human brain.

For the vast majority of human history, the world was a very dangerous place. Our ancestors didn't worry about unread emails or school theme days. They worried about being eaten. If a bush rustled in the tall grass, they didn't have the luxury of sitting down to "reflect" on whether it was the wind or a leopard. The ones who stopped to think didn't survive.

The ones who lived were the ones whose brains developed a lightning-fast, automatic alarm system. This system is located in the oldest part of our brain, often called the "reptilian brain" or the limbic system. Its job is simple: scanning for threats.

When this alarm sounds, it triggers the **Stress Response**. Knowing this can help women feel empowered, understanding their body's reactions as natural and manageable.

In a life-or-death moment, you don't need to be able to do math or remember your mother-in-law's birthday. You need to run, fight, or hide.

This worked beautifully for our ancestors. They would see the leopard; their bodies would catch fire with adrenaline; they would run to safety; and then, this is the key part, the leopard would be gone. Once they were safe back at the cave, their body would realize the threat had passed. They would shake, cry, rest, and their nervous system would return to its baseline "calm" state.

The problem is that the human brain hasn't had a significant hardware update in about 50,000 years. We are running ancient survival software on modern hardware.

Your brain cannot tell the difference between a leopard in the grass and a "We need to talk" text from your boss. It cannot tell the difference between a life-threatening famine and you forgetting to buy milk for the third time this week. To your ancient alarm system, stress is stress. But you can learn techniques like deep breathing, mindfulness, or grounding exercises to help signal to your brain that the threat has passed, allowing your nervous system to relax.

## Meet the Guardian

This is where we meet Dr. Aris. She isn't a historical figure from a textbook; she is a modern neuroscientist who has spent her life studying why women like Sarah feel so "on edge." Dr. Aris often explains the brain using a simple metaphor: The Guardian and The Librarian.

- **The Librarian** (your prefrontal cortex) is the part of you that keeps the files organized. She handles the schedules, the budgets, and the polite conversations. She likes order, logic, and long-term planning.

- **The Guardian** (your amygdala) is the part of you that stands at the gate. She doesn't care about the files. She only cares about safety. She is loud, fast, and very reactive.

In a healthy life, the Librarian is in charge most of the time. But when you are depleted, when you are chronically short on sleep, overwhelmed by the mental load, and carrying the emotional weight of everyone around you, the Librarian gets exhausted. She starts to make mistakes. She drops files.

When the Guardian sees the Librarian struggling, she gets worried. She thinks, *If the Librarian can't handle the files, we must be in danger.* So, The Guardian pushes the Librarian out of the chair and takes over.

This is why Sarah "glitched" in the grocery store. The Guardian was in the chair. When the shopping cart bumped her, The Guardian didn't see a polite neighbor; she saw a "threat to the perimeter." She flooded Sarah's body with fight-or-flight chemicals. Sarah's rage wasn't a character flaw; it was a survival response. Her "shutdown" in the car wasn't laziness; it was the "freeze" response, the body's last-ditch effort to play dead when it feels it can no longer fight or flee.

## The Window of Tolerance

When Dr. Aris talks to women in Sarah's position, she uses the concept of the **Window of Tolerance**.

Imagine a window. When you are inside this window, you can handle life's ups and downs. You might get annoyed, but you don't lose it. You might feel sad, but you can still function. This is your "green zone."

When you are rested and supported, your window is wide. You can handle the spilled juice, the traffic jam, and the work deadline all at once. But when you are depleted, your window begins to shrink. It becomes a tiny, narrow slit.

When your window is that small, the slightest breeze can knock you out of it.

- If you go "up" out of the window, you hit **Hyper-arousal**. This is the "Mom Snap." It's the yelling, the racing heart, the panic, and the feeling that you want to crawl out of your own skin.

- If you go "down" out of the window, you hit **Hypo-arousal**. This is the "Shutdown." It's the numbness, the "checked-out" feeling, and the inability to make a simple decision about what to have for dinner.

Sarah had spent three years living in a window that was only an inch wide. She was bouncing between screaming at the kids for dropping a shoe and staring blankly at the wall for an hour. She thought she was "unstable." But really, she was just "narrowed." Her system was so overloaded that it had no room left for even the smallest mistake.

## The Stress Response Cycle

There is a catch to our survival system that most of us were never taught. We think that once the stressful thing is over, the stress goes away. We think that if we finish the big project or survive the holidays, our bodies will automatically feel "calm."

But research, most famously highlighted by Drs. Emily and Amelia Nagoski show that the **stressor** and the **stress response** are distinct.

The *stressor* is the thing that causes the stress: the traffic, the toddler's tantrum, the looming bill. The *stress response* is a chemical reaction that happens inside your body.

Even if you solve the problem (the stressor), your body doesn't know it's safe until you "complete the cycle." Remember the cavewoman and the leopard? She didn't just escape the leopard; she ran, she breathed hard, she reached her tribe, she hugged them, and she finally exhaled. Those physical actions told her brain: *The danger is over. You can stop the adrenaline now.*

In our modern lives, we solve the stressors, but we never finish the cycle. We finish the stressful work call and immediately start making dinner.

We survive the chaotic morning drop-off and dive immediately into our inboxes. We are like a car that is constantly being revved in neutral. The engine is screaming, the heat is rising, but we aren't going anywhere.

This "incomplete stress" hangs around in your body. It settles in your shoulders, your jaw, and your gut. It builds up day after day, year after year, until you reach a state of **Chronic Depletion**. Your brain starts to think that "High Alert" is the only way to live. It forgets how to find the "off" switch.

## Why You Can't "Think" Your Way Out

This is the part that Sarah found most frustrating. She was a project manager! She was a problem solver! She tried to talk herself out of her panic. She would tell herself, *Sarah, it's just a grocery store. Calm down. You're being ridiculous.*

But here is the biological reality: You cannot talk to The Guardian. The Guardian doesn't speak English. She doesn't understand logic. She only speaks the language of the body.

When you are "activated," when you are in that hyper-arousal state, the part of your brain that understands words is literally offline. Trying to use logic to stop a panic attack is like trying to use a spreadsheet to stop a fire. You have to use water. You have to speak to your nervous system in its own language.

## The Cost of the "Good Girl" Script

For women, this biological struggle is made even worse by our cultural programming. From a young age, most women are taught the "Good Girl" script: be helpful, be quiet, be pleasant, and don't make a scene.

When a man feels the fight-or-flight response, society often permits him to "fight." He can be aggressive or loud, and it's seen as a sign of stress or strength. But when a woman feels that same surge of adrenaline, she is told to "keep it together."

This creates a massive internal conflict. Your biology is screaming at you to run or yell, but your social programming is telling you to smile and say "No problem!" This is a special kind of stress called **Fawning**. It's a survival response where you try to appease the "threat" by being extra nice or helpful.

Sarah realized she did this every single day. When her boss asked her to take on an extra project she didn't have time for, her heart would race (Flight), her stomach would knot (Fight), but her mouth would say, "Sure, I can handle that!" (Fawn).

Fawning is exhausting. It takes all your remaining mental energy to hide how you are really feeling. It's like trying to hold a beach ball underwater. Eventually, your arms get tired, and the ball is going to fly up and hit you in the face. This is often what leads to the "Mom Snap." It's not that you are a mean person; you just ran out of energy to keep the beach ball submerged.

## Your Sensitivity is Data

After months of feeling like she was failing, Sarah had a breakthrough during a conversation with a friend who understood the nervous system. Her friend said something that changed everything: "Sarah, your brain isn't betraying you. It's trying to save you. You're not 'too sensitive.' You're just highly tuned to a system that is currently toxic."

This is the "Aha!" moment. Your symptoms, the jaw clenching, the forgetfulness, the sudden rage, the deep fatigue, are not signs that you are broken. They are **data**.

- The "Mom Snap" is data that your boundaries have been crossed for too long.

- The "Brain Fog" is data that your Librarian is overworked and needs a break.

- The "Shutdown" in the car is data that your system is so overloaded that it had to pull the emergency brake to keep you from crashing.

When you stop seeing your stress as a personal failure and start seeing it as a biological signal, everything changes. You stop asking, *What is wrong with me?* and start asking, *What does my nervous system need right now to feel safe?* This shift from judgment to curiosity is where true healing begins.

## You Can Rewire the Alarm

The most beautiful thing about the human brain is its plasticity. It is not set in stone. Just as you "taught" your brain to stay on high alert through years of over-extension, you can teach it to find the way back to calm.

You don't need a week at a spa to do this. You don't need to quit your job or move to the woods. You need to start speaking the language of your body in small, 30-second increments.

When you feel yourself leaving the Window of Tolerance, you don't need a lecture. You need a **Reset**. You need to show The Guardian that there is no leopard.

Sarah started doing this in small ways. When she felt the "surge" in her chest during a difficult work call, she would press her feet firmly into the floor. She would feel the weight of her body in the chair. This is a "grounding" technique. It tells the brain: *You are here. You are solid. You are safe.*

She learned that she could manually override her stress response by changing her breathing. She learned about the **Physiological Sigh**, a specific breathing pattern that scientists have found is the fastest way to lower your heart rate.

## The Physiological Sigh

You will use this tool today. Not when you are in the middle of a breakdown, but right now, while you are reading this. And then, you are going to use it the next time you feel your jaw tighten, or your heart speed up.

This is a biological "hack" that speaks directly to your parasympathetic nervous system, the "rest and digest" part of your brain.

1. **Inhale deeply through your nose.**

2. **At the very top of that breath, take a second, shorter "sip" of air through your nose** to fully inflate the tiny sacs in your lungs.

3. **Exhale slowly through your mouth** and make a "whoosh" sound. Make the exhale twice as long as the inhale.

Do this three times in a row.

When you do this, you send a physical signal to your brain that says, *"The threat has passed." You can stand down.* It is a way of manually pulling The Guardian out of the chair and letting The Librarian take a breath.

Sarah started doing the Physiological Sigh before she walked into her house after work. She called it her "Entry Ritual." It took forty-five seconds. In those forty-five seconds, she finished the stress cycle of the workday, so she didn't carry it into the evening. She wasn't "perfectly calm," but she was back inside her Window of Tolerance. She was no longer a "glitch" in a parking lot; she was a woman with a tool.

## The Long Game

Understanding the science of your stress is the first step toward reclaiming your life. It takes the shame out of the equation. You aren't a "messy" woman or a "bad" mother. You are a biological being with a highly sophisticated survival system that has been pushed to its limit.

But knowing *why* you feel this way is only half the battle. Now that we've looked at the biology of your internal world, we have to look at the reality of your external world. Even with the best breathing techniques in the world, it is hard to stay calm when you are carrying a load no one else sees.

In the next section, we are going to pull back the curtain on the "mental load." We are going to look at the invisible work that keeps you in survival mode, the labor of tracking, planning, and worrying that is currently eating your brain alive.

Your brain isn't betraying you, but your schedule might be. It's time to name the load so you can finally start to put it down.

# Chapter Three

# The Load Nobody Sees

## Invisible Labor and the Women Who Carry It

The house was finally quiet. It was 9:45 p.m. on a Sunday, and the only sound was the low, rhythmic hum of the dishwasher in the kitchen. Sarah Miller sat on the second step of the staircase, a single sock in her hand, staring at the front door. The hallway light cast a long, soft shadow across the hardwood. For a few seconds, it felt like the world had stopped spinning. The kids were asleep. Her husband, Mark, was upstairs finishing a book. The "To-Do" list for Monday was written and sitting on the counter.

By all accounts, this was the moment of rest she had been chasing all week. She should have felt a sense of accomplishment. Instead, she felt a strange, cold tightness in her chest.

She looked at the sock. It belonged to her eight-year-old, Leo. It was a soccer sock, stained with grass at the heel. Seeing it didn't just remind her of laundry; it triggered a cascade of data points. *Leo has practice on Tuesday. Tuesday is also my regional sales call day. If the practice is at 5:00, I need to leave work by 4:30. If I leave at 4:30, I won't have time to prep the chicken. I need to move the chicken to the fridge tonight. Also, Leo mentioned his cleats were tight. I need to check the size. If he needs new ones, I have to find a store that's open late tomorrow because Wednesday is a game day.*

In the silence of her beautiful, quiet home, Sarah's brain was screaming. She wasn't just holding a sock; she was holding a logistical map of the next seventy-two hours. Recognizing this ongoing mental effort can give women confidence to set boundaries and practice letting go of control, which is vital for true calm.

This is the weight of the load nobody sees, known as invisible labor, which includes mental, emotional, and social work that keeps a family, household, and career functioning. Yet it has no line item in the budget and no "thank you" in the performance review. Recognizing this invisible labor is key to understanding the need for redistribution and change.

## The Manager and the Doer

To understand why Sarah felt so heavy while doing nothing, we have to look at a concept that gained global attention through a simple comic by a French artist named Emma. The comic, titled *You Should Have Asked*, perfectly captured a dynamic that plays out in millions of homes every day.

The story goes like this: A woman is frantically cooking dinner while managing two children. A pot boils over, a child cries, and the chaos peaks. Her husband, sitting nearby, looks up and says, "You should have asked me to help."

On the surface, it sounds like a kind offer. But as Emma pointed out, the phrase "You should have asked" implies that the woman is the **Manager** of the household, and the partner is a **Volunteer**.

As the Manager, you are responsible for the "Mental Load." You have to identify the task, delegate it, and then follow up to make sure it was done correctly. If Sarah asks Mark to "help" with the groceries, she still has to be the one who checks the pantry, writes the list, and remembers that they are out of the specific bread the toddler will actually eat. Mark does the physical labor of driving to the store and paying, but Sarah does the cognitive labor of ensuring the family doesn't starve.

The "Doer" gets to finish a task and be done with it. The "Manager" is never done, because her job isn't the task. It's the oversight of all tasks.

## The Five Faces of Invisible Work

Most women think they are just "stressed about the house." But when we break down the invisible load, we see that it's actually a complex system of five different types of labor. Naming them is the first step in realizing you aren't "crazy" for being tired. You are simply working five jobs at once.

### 1. Cognitive Labor (The Tracking)

This is the practical, logistical management of life. It's knowing when the car needs an oil change, remembering that the dog needs heartworm pills on the 15th, and keeping track of the school calendar. That's the "Human Sticky Note" role Sarah played. It's the constant scanning of the environment to see what needs to be maintained.

### 2. Emotional Labor (The Thermostat)

This is the work of managing everyone's feelings around you. When Sarah noticed that Leo seemed "off" after school, she spent thirty minutes gently asking questions to see if he was being bullied. When Mark was stressed about a deadline, she adjusted her tone to be more supportive and kept the house extra quiet. Women are socialized to be the "Emotional Thermostat" of the room. They adjust themselves to keep everyone else at a comfortable temperature.

### 3. Social Labor (The Connection)

This is the work of maintaining the "Village." It's buying wedding gifts, RSVPing to birthday parties, checking in on aging parents, and making sure the neighbors feel seen. If a holiday card gets sent, it's usually because a woman tracked the addresses and bought the stamps. This labor keeps the family connected to the world, but it takes an enormous amount of "social battery" to manage.

## 4. Aesthetic Labor, or How It Feels

This is the pressure to keep the home looking and feeling like a "haven." It's noticing the clutter on the counter, the dust on the baseboards, or the fact that the living room feels "stale." It's the work of keeping the house looking right. Even if a woman isn't the one doing the cleaning, she is often the one *to notice the mess, which creates a constant* low-level visual stress.

## 5. Anticipatory Labor (The Future)

As we touched on in Chapter 1, this is the chess game. It's the mental energy of predicting problems before they happen. It's buying the next size up in boots during the summer sale, so you aren't caught off guard by the first snow. It's the "What If" engine that never stops running.

# The Compound Interest of "Small Things"

This labor is so exhausting because it has **Compound Interest**.

If you had to do just one of these things, it would be easy. If your only job were to remember to buy lightbulbs, you wouldn't be "depleted." But when you are tracking 400 "small things" simultaneously, your brain loses the ability to distinguish between a small thing and a big thing.

Each tiny piece of invisible labor leaves what psychologists call "Cognitive Residue." When you switch from a work email to thinking about a child's dental appointment, a small piece of your attention stays stuck on the dental appointment. By the end of the day, your brain is covered in these sticky bits of unfinished thoughts. This is why Sarah felt "glitched" in the grocery store. Her RAM (random access memory) was full. There was no room left for a stranger bumping her cart.

## The Loneliness of the Unseen

Perhaps the hardest part of invisible labor isn't the work itself, but the loneliness of it. Because the work is invisible, it is often unthanked.

When Mark finishes mowing the lawn, he can look back and see a clear result. He feels a sense of completion. Sarah can say, "I spent three hours managing the family," but there is nothing to show for it. The house looks the same. The kids are still just... kids.

When your labor isn't seen, you start to feel invisible yourself. You start to feel like a "utility" rather than a person. You aren't "Sarah, the woman who loves hiking and mystery novels"; you are "The Person Who Keeps Everything Running."

This creates a lot of resentment. Resentment isn't a sign that you don't love your family; it's a biological response to an unfair distribution of energy. It is your system's way of saying, *I am giving more than I am receiving, and I am running out of fuel.* If left unaddressed, this depletion doesn't just lead to exhaustion; it eventually erodes the very foundation of the connection you are trying to protect.

## Making the Invisible Visible

If you want to find calm, you have to stop being the only person who knows how the "magic" happens. You have to move from Manager to Partner. This isn't about "getting more help," it's about **Redistributing the Load**.

Here are three practical techniques to start making your invisible labor visible today.

## 1. The "I Noticed" Audit

Most partners and coworkers don't ignore the invisible load because they are mean; they ignore it because they literally do not see it. They have been "socially blinded" to the details because you have handled them so well for so long.

Try the **"I Noticed" Audit** for twenty-four hours. Keep a running list on your phone of every time you "notice" something that needs to be done.

- *I noticed the toilet paper is down to two rolls.*

- *I noticed the school email said tomorrow is "Purple Shirt Day."*

- *I noticed the printer is low on ink.*

At the end of the day, look at the list. Do not use it as a weapon to yell at your partner. Use it as **data**. This list is the "job description" you have been fulfilling without a salary. Simply seeing it on paper can provide a massive sense of validation. It proves that your exhaustion is logical.

## 2. The "Minimum Viable Magic" Filter

We often perform invisible labor to create "magic" for our loved ones. We want the holidays to be perfect, the birthdays to be special, and the home to be cozy. But we have to ask: *At what cost to my nervous system?*

Apply the **Minimum Viable Magic** filter to your social and aesthetic labor.

- Do the kids need a three-tier themed cake, or would they be just as happy with a grocery store sheet cake and a happy mom?

- Does the guest room need fresh flowers, or does it just need clean sheets?

When you lower the bar for "magic," you reclaim the cognitive energy that was being used for curation. You permit yourself to exist in a "good enough" environment.

## 3. The "Out Loud" Validation

Invisible labor stays invisible because we do it in our heads. To break the cycle, start narrating your mental load out loud, not as a complaint, but as a statement of fact.

Instead of just thinking, *I need to remember to call the pediatrician,* say it out loud: "I'm currently using my mental energy to remember to call the pediatrician tomorrow."

When Sarah started doing this, the atmosphere in the kitchen changed. Mark would hear her say, "I'm mentally tracking the logistics for the weekend," and he would suddenly realize that her "sitting on the couch" wasn't actually rest. It was work. It allowed him to say, "I can take that off your plate. I'll handle the weekend logistics."

## The "Sock" Discovery Moment

Back on that Sunday night, Sarah looked down at Leo's soccer sock. Usually, she would have stood up, walked to the laundry room, checked the cleats, and spent the next hour in a spiral of anticipatory labor.

But Sarah had been reading about the "Labor of Noticing." She took a breath. She didn't move.

When Mark came downstairs to get a glass of water, she held up the sock. "Hey Mark," she said quietly. "I just noticed this sock. It reminded me that Leo has practice on Tuesday, he needs his cleats checked for size, and I have a conflict with my work call."

Mark paused. He looked at the sock, then at Sarah. "Oh, man. I totally forgot about the soccer schedule."

"I know," Sarah said. "Because I've been the only one tracking it. I'm feeling really overwhelmed by the logistics of Tuesday. Can you take over the 'Soccer Plate' entirely? From checking the shoes to getting him there?"

Mark didn't get defensive. He didn't say, "You should have asked." He saw the exhaustion in her eyes and realized that the "magic" of Leo getting to soccer on time had been wearing Sarah out.

"Yeah," Mark said, taking the sock from her hand. "I've got the soccer plate. You can delete that from your brain."

Sarah sat on the stairs and watched him walk into the kitchen. For the first time in years, she felt a tiny "click" in her head. It was the sound of one tab finally closing. She didn't check the laundry. She didn't check her email. She just sat there and listened to the dishwasher.

## The Reality of This Is Not a "Fix"

Redistributing the load is not a one-time event. It is a slow, often uncomfortable process of retraining yourself and the people around you. You will feel the urge to "check in" on the tasks you've handed off. You will feel the "guilt" of seeing someone else struggle with a plate you used to spin perfectly.

But you must remember: **Your peace is more important than a perfectly spun plate.**

If Mark forgets the water bottle for soccer practice, it is not a disaster. It is a learning moment for him and a "growing pain" for the family. If you step in to "save" the situation, you are taking the load back. You are telling your brain that it is still your job to notice everything.

True calm requires the courage to let someone else imperfectly manage things. It requires you to be "brave enough to be bored" while someone else figures out the lightbulbs.

## The Path Forward

Naming the invisible labor is like turning on the lights in a room you've been cleaning in the dark. It's overwhelming at first to see how much dust has collected, but you can finally see where to start.

You are not "lazy" for wanting to stop being the Manager. You are not "failing" because you don't want to track the birthday gifts for your in-laws. You are a person with limited cognitive fuel, and you are choosing to save some of it for yourself.

But even when we name the load, we often find ourselves unable to put it down. We feel like we "should" be able to handle it. We see other women on social media who seem to have the "magic" and the "calm" all at once. We tell ourselves that if we just had better "self-care," we wouldn't feel so depleted.

In the next part of our journey, we are going to look at why the "self-care" you've been sold is actually making you more tired. We're going to look at why a bubble bath can't fix a nervous system that is on fire, and what actually works to bring a woman back to life.

Because once you've named the load, you need the permission to rest, specifically the kind of rest that actually reaches your soul rather than just looking good in a photo.

# Chapter Four

# Why Self-Care Isn't Working

## And What Actually Does

In 1948, the World Health Organization was established to tackle the physical diseases that had ravaged the globe after years of war, but in the quiet corners of suburban New Jersey, a different kind of problem was brewing. While medical pioneers were celebrating the discovery of antibiotics and the polio vaccine, a woman named Shirley stood in her kitchen, surrounded by the very "labor-saving" gadgets (the electric toaster, the automatic washing machine, the vacuum cleaner) that were supposed to set her free. Despite the gleaming chrome and the promise of modern efficiency, Shirley felt a hollow, bone-deep fatigue that no amount of sleep could touch. She was living in the "Golden Age" of the American housewife, yet she described herself as a "clock-watcher." She waited for the hours to tick by until she could close her eyes, only to wake up and feel the same.

The world was focused on the body's health, but it was ignoring the erosion of the self. Shirley's doctors told her to take a "nerve pill" or perhaps a longer bath. They offered her the 1950s version of self-care: a sedative and a suggestion to buy a prettier dress. They treated her exhaustion as a personal malfunction rather than a response to a life that had become a series of performances for others. This was the birth of the "Self-Care Industrial Complex," a system that tells women that the solution to burnout is to change consumer habits or to escape their own reality temporarily. Instead, sustainable self-care involves meaningful, guilt-free habits that honor your limits and needs.

Sarah Miller sat in her car. She clutched a crumpled receipt for an expensive lavender-scented candle and a high-end face mask. She had spent forty dollars at a boutique during her lunch break because a social media post told her she "deserved a treat." She was hiding in her driveway, the engine idling, because the thought of walking through her front door felt like stepping into a wind tunnel of demands. She looked at the candle in the bag. It was supposed to represent "calm," but as she sat there, she realized that lighting a candle while her brain was still tracking two different school schedules and a project budget was like putting a decorative band-aid on a broken leg.

She had tried the apps. She had a drawer full of journals with "Gratitude" embossed in gold foil. She had even tried a 5:00 a.m. yoga routine that lasted exactly three days before she realized that waking up an hour earlier just meant she was exhausted for sixty more minutes a day. Every time a self-care routine failed to make her feel better, Sarah didn't blame the routine. She blamed herself. She assumed she was "bad at relaxing." She felt like a failure at the very thing that was supposed to save her from feeling like a failure.

## The Self-Care Industrial Complex

The reason Sarah felt she was failing at self-care is that the modern definition of the term has hijacked it. What began as a radical political concept, the idea that marginalized people must care for their own health because the system will not, has been rebranded into a multi-billion-dollar industry. We are told that "self-care" is something you buy, something you schedule, or something you perform for an audience. To truly restore yourself, it's essential to recognize and challenge these societal pressures and instead embrace self-care practices that feel authentic and guilt-free.

This version of self-care is what Dr. Aris calls "Maintenance Mimicry." It looks like restoration, but it is just another to-do list item. If your self-care requires you to "find time" that you don't have, to spend money you're stressed about, or to learn a new skill, it isn't care. It's a job. To avoid this trap, women need to learn to listen to their bodies and feelings, recognizing when their routines genuinely restore energy rather than just ticking boxes to meet societal standards.

When you are depleted, your brain treats a scheduled "yoga hour" the same way it treats a dentist appointment. It is a commitment you have to keep, a logistical hurdle to clear, and a standard you have to meet. If you aren't "present" during the yoga, or if you spend the whole time thinking about the grocery list, you walk away feeling more stressed than when you started. You have failed at the "rest," and the Guardian in your brain sees that failure as one more reason to stay on high alert. The rest should be guilt-free and unearned, allowing women to feel safe taking space for themselves without shame.

True restoration is really about what you stop doing rather than what you do. Embracing self-preservation can empower women to prioritize their well-being and feel validated in their choices.

## The Four Types of Rest

To move beyond the face-mask-and-bubble-bath trap, we have to understand that depletion isn't just one thing. When you say, "I'm tired," you might be experiencing four very different types of emptiness. Each one requires a different kind of refill.

- **Physical Rest** is the most obvious, but it's often the one we misunderstand. It isn't just sleep. It is the absence of physical demand. For Sarah, physical rest didn't mean going for a "restorative" walk; it meant sitting in a chair and not having a toddler climb on her for ten minutes. It is the state of being "untouched."

- **Mental Rest** is the quietening of the "Librarian." This is the rest from noticing, tracking, and planning. If you are sleeping but still dreaming about your spreadsheet, you are not getting mental rest. This requires a "brain dump," literally getting the information out of your head and onto paper so your brain can stop holding the files.

- **Emotional Rest** is the freedom to stop performing. It is the space where you don't have to be "pleasant," "helpful," or "on." For women, this is the hardest to find. We are almost always "on" for someone, like a child, a partner, a boss, or even the cashier at the store. Emotional rest happens when you can be authentic, even if that authenticity is grumpy, tired, or silent.

- **Social Rest** is the difference between relationships that drain you and relationships that refill you. Most of Sarah's social life was "Social Labor," including organizing playdates, visiting in-laws, or attending work happy hours. Social rest is the presence of people who require nothing from you, people in whose presence you can be entirely still.

## The Permission Problem

In the early 1900s, a neurologist named George Beard coined the term "neurasthenia" to describe a state of nervous exhaustion caused by the "frenetic pace" of modern life. His treatment for men usually involved "the West Cure," sending them out to ranches to hunt and be rugged. For women, he prescribed "the Rest Cure," forcing them to stay in bed for weeks, forbidden from reading, writing, or even speaking.

While the "Rest Cure" was a nightmare of control, it pointed to a simple truth: women were rarely permitted to stop unless they were physically incapacitated. One hundred years later, and we have internalized this. We feel that rest must be "earned." We tell ourselves we can sit down *after* the laundry is folded, *after* the emails are sent, *after* the house is quiet.

The problem, as Sarah discovered, is that in modern life, the laundry is never fully folded and the house is never truly quiet. If you wait until the work is done to rest, you will be waiting until you are dead.

This is the "Rest Guilt." It is a physiological response. When Sarah tried to sit on the couch while the kitchen was messy, her Guardian would scream. It felt "unsafe" to be still while there were threats (messy counters) in her environment. She felt like a "bad mom" or a "lazy wife."

To overcome this, we have to reframe restoration as **Self-Preservation**. It is not a luxury; it is survival-level maintenance. You wouldn't feel "guilty" for putting gas in your car or charging your phone. You recognize that without fuel, the machine stops. You are the machine.

## Self-Care vs. Self-Preservation

The shift from "Self-Care" to "Self-Preservation" is the turning point for the depleted woman. Self-care is a "want"; self-preservation is a "need."

When Sarah started looking at her life this way, her choices changed. Instead of trying to force herself into a twenty-minute meditation (Self-Care), she started taking five minutes to sit in the dark in her pantry when she felt "touched out" (Self-Preservation). The pantry was quiet. No one was looking at her. It wasn't "pretty," it wouldn't make a good photo for social media, and it didn't cost a dime. But it gave her nervous system the specific silence it was begging for.

Self-preservation is about identifying the "leaks" in your bucket and plugging them. If you are spending thirty minutes every night scrolling through social media and feeling worse about your life, that is a leak. Plugging that leak by putting your phone in another room isn't "self-care"; it's protecting your limited mental resources.

## Your Personal Restoration Menu

Because every woman's depletion is different, there is no "one size fits all" solution. Sarah needed a menu of options that didn't require her to "find time," but instead let her "stow away" into moments of peace.

She created a grid of activities based on the time she had available. She stopped looking for an hour and started looking for sixty seconds.

- **The 1-Minute Micro-Rest**: A physiological sigh, a glass of water drunk in total silence, or simply closing her eyes while the microwave ran.

- **The 10-Minute Transition**: Driving the long way home from work to listen to a song she loved, or sitting on the porch before going inside.

- **The 30-Minute Boundary**: Telling Mark, "I am going into the bedroom for thirty minutes. Unless the house is on fire, do not knock."

The key to the "Restoration Menu" is that nothing on it can feel like a chore. If "reading a book" felt like something she *should* do, she crossed it off. If "staring at the ceiling" was what her brain actually wanted, she did that.

## Resting Without Earning It

The most radical act a depleted woman can perform is to rest when things are still undone. It is a rebellion against the productivity cult that tells us our value is tied to our output.

Sarah tried a small experiment on a Tuesday night. The dishes were in the sink. The mail was piled on the counter. Usually, she would spend forty-five minutes clearing it all before allowing herself to sit. Instead, she looked at the pile and said to herself, "The mail will be there tomorrow. My nervous system needs me now."

She sat on the couch and stared out the window for fifteen minutes. The world did not end. Her children were fine. Mark didn't even notice the mail. The only thing that changed was the internal pressure in her chest. By permitting herself to rest without earning it, she was teaching her Guardian that she was safe even with an unfinished task.

She was widening her Window of Tolerance by proving that "imperfection" wasn't a threat to her survival.

## The Vision of a Restored Life

When you stop trying to "do" self-care and start practicing self-preservation, the fog begins to lift. You start to realize that the version of you that is "always on" isn't actually the best version of you. It's just the busiest.

Imagine a life where you don't wake up already calculating how much you have to "achieve" before you're allowed to stop. Imagine a version of yourself that can see a messy kitchen and feel zero spike in cortisol because you know that your worth isn't in the shine of the granite.

This isn't a life of laziness. It is a life of **Sustainable Energy**. When you are restored, you are a better mother, a better partner, and a better professional, not because you are doing more, but because you are bringing a regulated nervous system to the table. You are no longer reacting out of panic; you are responding with presence.

Sarah Miller isn't "fixed" yet. She still has days when she hides in the car. But she no longer feels like she has to buy her way out of exhaustion. She knows that her calm is a right, not a reward. She is learning that the most important "plate" she is spinning is herself, and that if she breaks, all the other plates go down anyway.

But even with the right kind of rest and a better understanding of her brain, Sarah still found herself hitting a wall. She would rest, she would breathe, and then, at the first sign of a child's tantrum or a sharp email, her body would "ignite" again. She felt like she was clearing the stress, but she wasn't clearing the *cycle*.

She was resting her mind, but her body was still holding onto the "vibration" of the threat. She realized that sitting still was only half the battle. To truly find calm, she had to learn how to move the stress *through* her, to literally flush the adrenaline out of her muscles so it didn't sit there and fester. She had to learn the difference between being still and being finished.

# Chapter Five

# Completing the Stress Cycle

## How to Actually Calm Down

"I just don't understand why you're still so angry about it," Mark said, his voice reaching that specific level of calm that feels like a provocation. "The car is fine. We aren't going to be late. The rabbit is in the house. It's over, Sarah. Why can't you just let it go?"

Sarah stood at the kitchen island, her hand still white-knuckled around her car keys. Her chest felt like a giant fist was squeezing it. "I know it's over, Mark. I know the car is in park. I'm not 'angry' at the car. I'm just... I can't stop my heart from doing this."

"Doing what?"

"Thumping. Vibrating. I feel like I'm vibrating. I want to jump out of my skin."

"Take a deep breath," he suggested, already turning back to his laptop. "Just relax. It's a beautiful day."

Sarah watched him settle back into his work, his shoulders loose, his breathing steady. He had processed the "threat" of the rolling car, realized it was gone, and his body had reset. He was finished. Recognizing this can help you feel more secure that your body can find calm again, which is essential for your well-being.

## The Gap Between Solving and Finishing

Most of us live our lives in the gap Sarah was standing in. We spend our days solving problems, the late bill, the broken dishwasher, the awkward work email, and we assume that because the problem is "solved," our stress should be gone. We treat stress like a math equation: once you find the answer, the work is over.

But your body doesn't do math. Your body does biology.

As we saw in the science of survival mode, your nervous system triggers a massive chemical reaction to help you survive a threat. This is the **Stress Response Cycle**. It has a beginning (the threat appears), a middle (your body reacts), and an end (your body realizes it is safe). Recognizing and completing this cycle is essential to recover from stress fully, so your body can reset, and you can feel calmer.

The tragedy of the depleted woman is that we are world-class at managing the *beginning* and the *middle, but we struggle with the end*. We see the threat. We react with lightning speed. We juggle the plates. We solve the crisis. But we rarely get to the *end*. We solve the problem, but we don't finish the cycle.

Imagine you are a gazelle on the savannah. A lion chases you. You run with every ounce of strength you have. Your heart is pounding, your muscles are screaming, and your brain is flooded with adrenaline. You reach the safety of the herd. The lion gives up.

In that moment, the "stressor" (the lion) is gone. But the "stress" (the adrenaline and cortisol) is still inside the gazelle. If the gazelle just stood perfectly still and tried to "relax" the way Mark suggested to Sarah, the chemicals would sit in its muscles and fester. Instead, the gazelle does something instinctual. It shakes. It trembles. It breathes heavily. It completes a physical sequence that tells its nervous system: *The chase is over. You survived. You can stop the alarm.*

When we solve a problem at work or manage a family crisis, we usually move on to the next task immediately. We finish the stressful meeting and go straight to a grocery list. We survive a chaotic morning and go straight to a spreadsheet. We are "safe," but our bodies are still holding the "lion" chemicals. We are revving our engines while the car is in park, and eventually the engine will burn out.

## The Six Proven Cycle Completers

If you want to move from "solved" to "finished," you have to speak the language of the body. You have to give your nervous system physical evidence that the "threat" is over. This is what Dr. Aris calls "Completing the Cycle."

Based on the work of researchers like the Nagoski sisters and decades of neurobiological data, there are six primary ways to flush stress out of your system. These methods give you tangible tools to actively release energy, helping you feel more in control of your stress and health.

### 1. Physical Activity

This is the most efficient way to complete the cycle. Even ninety seconds of jumping jacks or a brisk walk can help you feel empowered, showing your brain that you've responded to the threat and can now relax.

### 2. Breathing

We've talked about the Physiological Sigh, but any deep, slow breathing, especially when the exhale is longer than the inhale, works. This is the only part of your autonomic nervous system you can consciously control. When you slow your breath, you are manually overriding the "High Alert" signal. You are showing The Guardian that you can't possibly be in danger if you are breathing this slowly.

## 3. Positive Social Interaction

A brief, friendly interaction with another person tells your brain that the world is a safe place. This could be a joke with the grocery store clerk or a warm "hello" to a neighbor. It signals to your ancient brain that you are back with your "tribe" and the predator is gone.

## 4. Laughter

Not a polite chuckle, but a deep, belly-shaking laugh. Laughter is a physical release. It changes your brain chemistry and forces a deep exhale. This is why we often feel "weak" or "limp" after a massive laughing fit—that is the feeling of your nervous system finally dropping its guard.

## 5. Affection (The 20-Second Hug)

There is a specific biological shift that happens when we hold someone we trust for a long time. A quick "side-hug" won't do it. You need a full, chest-to-chest hug that lasts at least twenty seconds. During this time, your body releases oxytocin, your heart rate slows, and your brain receives the message: *I am home. I am protected.*

## 6. A Big Ol' Cry

Crying is a physical mechanism for processing stress. It is not a sign of weakness; it is a sign of a high-functioning nervous system. When you cry, you are literally expelling stress hormones through your tears. Have you ever noticed how you feel "scoured out" and exhausted but strangely calm after a massive sob? That is the sound of a stress cycle finally closing its doors.

# The Struggle of the "Frozen" Woman

The reason these techniques feel so hard for women like Sarah is that we have been taught to fear our own physical responses. We are told to "keep a lid on it." We worry that if we start crying, we'll never stop. We worry that if we start shaking or yelling, we'll look "crazy."

But when you suppress the physical completion of the cycle, you enter a state called **Functional Freeze**.

This is the state Sarah was in at the kitchen island. She was "functioning." She was standing, talking, planning. But she was "frozen" inside. Her body was stuck in a high-arousal state that had nowhere to go.

Think of your stress like a garden hose. The water is the adrenaline. When a stressor happens, the tap is turned on full blast. If you don't "complete the cycle," it's like putting your thumb over the end of the hose. The pressure builds and builds. The hose starts to vibrate. Eventually, the pressure is so high that the hose will either burst (The Mom Snap) or the connection to the tap will fail (The Shutdown).

The "struggle" isn't the stress itself; it's the pressure of the incomplete cycle. We spend so much energy trying to *hide* the fact that we are stressed that we have no energy left to *process* it.

# Dr. Aris and the "Tonic Immobility"

Dr. Aris often points to a fascinating and heartbreaking study of "tonic immobility" in animals. When a predator catches an animal and cannot fight or flee, it goes limp. It plays dead. This is a biological "last resort" to prevent pain and, hopefully, to trick the predator into loosening its grip.

Once the predator leaves, the animal doesn't just get up and go back to eating grass. It goes through a violent period of "thawing." It shakes, it pants, it convulses. It has to remove the "freeze" from its tissues before it can return to normal life.

As women, we often "play dead" emotionally. We go numb. We "grin and bear it." We push through the burnout. But we also need to "thaw." If you have spent years in a high-stress job or a demanding caregiving role, you are likely carrying a massive amount of "frozen" stress.

Completing the cycle is about more than handling today's traffic; it's about slowly thawing the years of "tonic immobility" that have settled in your bones.

## Mapping Your Stress Signals

To use these tools effectively, you have to know when the tap is on. Most of us are so disconnected from our bodies that we don't realize we are stressed until we are already screaming or crying. We miss the "Early Warning System."

Sarah started to realize that her body gave her clues long before she reached her breaking point.

- Her first signal was a specific tightness in the back of her neck, right where it met her skull.

- Her second signal was "looping thoughts." She would start checking her phone every thirty seconds for no reason.

- Her third signal was "sensory sensitivity." The sound of the dishwasher would suddenly feel like someone was scraping a fingernail across her brain.

By the time she reached the third signal, she was already outside her Window of Tolerance. She learned that if she could catch the first signal, the neck tightness, she could complete a "micro-cycle" before the pressure became dangerous.

She started doing "The Shake." When she felt that neck tension, she would go into the bathroom, lock the door, and literally shake her arms and legs for thirty seconds. It felt ridiculous. She felt like a wet dog. But she could feel the "vibration" in her chest start to settle. She was giving her Guardian the physical proof it needed to stand down.

# The 2 a.m. From Panic to Peace

Let's go back to the woman staring at the ceiling in the middle of the night. In the Introduction, we saw this woman caught in the "I need to be better" spiral. She was trying to solve her 2 a.m. panic with logic. She was making lists. She was blaming herself.

But panic at 2 a.m. is rarely about the things on your list. It is the sound of an uncompleted stress cycle from 2 p.m., finally catching up with you. Your body is quiet, the house is still, and your nervous system finally has the "space" to process the adrenaline you ignored all day. The "anxiety" you feel at night is often just the "leftover" energy of the day trying to find an exit.

When Sarah realized this, her 2 a.m. hours changed. Instead of making lists, she would get out of bed and do something physical. She would do ten slow wall-pushes or a series of deep, audible sighs. She stopped trying to "think" her way out of the panic and started "moving" her way through it.

She stopped asking, *What is wrong with my life?* and started asking, *What stress cycle did I leave open today?* By giving her body a physical way to close that loop, she finally gave her mind permission to rest.

## The Micro-Completion Practice

You don't need a "perfect" environment to complete a cycle. In fact, waiting for a perfect time is just another way to stay frozen. You have to learn to fit completion into the "transition moments" of your life.

- **The Car-to-House Transition**: Before you get out of your car after work or errands, do three Physiological Sighs. Feel your weight in the seat. This prevents you from bringing "driving stress" home.

- **The Work to Dinner Transition**: After you close your laptop, put on one song you love and dance, really dance, for three minutes. This tells your brain the "work lion" is gone.

- **The Bedtime Transition**: If you feel "wired but tired," do a 20-second hug with your partner or even a pet. If you live alone, use a weighted blanket or wrap yourself tightly in a towel after a shower. The physical pressure gives your brain the "safety" signal it's looking for.

Sarah Miller started treating these moments as non-negotiable. She realized that if she didn't spend three minutes completing the cycle, she would spend three hours feeling miserable. It was the most efficient "productivity hack" she had ever found, because it gave her back her ability to think clearly.

## That "Finished" Feeling

The goal of completing the cycle isn't to become "perfectly happy." It is about reaching the **Physiological Neutral state**.

You know that feeling when you finally get into a warm bed after a long day of travel? Or the way your body feels after a long swim? That is the "finished" feeling. It is a sense of heaviness that is also light. It is the feeling of your muscles finally letting go of their "readiness."

When you reach this state, your "Librarian" comes back online. You can look at your to-do list and actually prioritize. You can hear your child's request for a snack without wanting to cry. You haven't changed the world; you've just changed the state of the person living in it.

## Resist? "I Don't Have Time for This"

The biggest hurdle for the depleted woman isn't the technique; it's the belief that she doesn't have the "right" to spend three minutes on herself while things are still undone.

Sarah struggled with this. She felt "guilty" for dancing in the kitchen while Mark was starting dinner. She felt "silly" for shaking her arms in the bathroom. She felt like she was "wasting time."

But we must remember the lesson of the garden hose. If you don't take the time to release the pressure, the hose will burst. The three minutes you spend completing the stress cycle are an investment that prevents the three-hour "Mom Snap" or the three-day "Shutdown."

Completing the cycle is a gift you give the people you love. When you are "finished," you are present. When you are "frozen," you are just a ghost moving through the house. Your family doesn't need a version of you that is perfectly efficient; they need a version of you that is biologically safe.

## The Wisdom Distilled

Sarah Miller stood in her kitchen two weeks after the "car incident." The sink was full of dishes, and Leo was currently complaining that he couldn't find his favorite blue shirt. Usually, this combination of sensory input and logistical failure would have sent her into a spiral of rage.

But Sarah noticed the tightness in her neck. She caught the first signal.

"I'll find the shirt in a second, Leo," she said, her voice steady. She walked to the hallway, leaned her hands against the wall, and did five slow, heavy wall-pushups. She exhaled with a loud "Whoosh."

She felt the "vibration" in her chest settle. She wasn't "happy" about the dishes, but she was finished with the stress of the morning. She walked back into the kitchen, found the blue shirt (it was under the couch), and started the dishes without feeling like she was about to explode.

She had learned the secret that would eventually lead her back to herself. It was a principle she wrote on a Post-it note and stuck to her bathroom mirror:

**The problem is in your life, but the stress is in your body. You cannot think your way to calm; you must move your way there.**

By learning to complete the stress cycle, Sarah had finally found the "off" switch for her survival mode. She was no longer a gazelle running forever from a lion she couldn't see. She was a woman who knew how to come home to herself.

But as Sarah began to clear the biological stress from her body, she bumped into a new, even more stubborn obstacle. She realized that even when her nervous system was calm, she was still holding herself to standards that were physically impossible to meet. She found that her "Librarian" was a perfectionist who didn't know how to say "enough."

She was clearing the stress, but she was still producing the stress through a deep-seated need to be perfect, pleasant, and "good." She realized that if she wanted to stay calm, she had to do more than shake off the adrenaline; she had to dismantle the "Good Girl" programming that was keeping the tap turned on in the first place.

She had to learn the art of being "enough" in a world that never stops asking for more.

# Chapter Six

# The Art of the Enough

## Perfectionism, People-Pleasing, and the Women They Exhaust

S arah Miller was in the middle of her kitchen at 11:45 p.m., staring at a batch of twenty-four cupcakes that were, by any logical standard, a disaster. They weren't burnt, and they weren't raw. They were... lumpy. The frosting, which she had tried to dye a very specific shade of "ocean breeze" for her son Leo's school bake sale, had separated into a grainy, oily mess that resembled wet cement.

Three weeks later, Sarah would be sitting on her back porch with a cold glass of water, watching the sunset and feeling a sense of peace so deep it felt like a physical weight had been lifted from her chest. She would look back at the "Cupcake Crisis" and laugh, but in that midnight moment, she wasn't laughing. She was crying. She was leaning against the counter, her eyes stinging from exhaustion, convinced that these lumpy cupcakes were proof that she was a failure as a mother, a professional, and a human being.

The "Ocean Breeze" disaster didn't start in the kitchen. It started three days earlier when Sarah's brain had whispered a very dangerous thought: *It has to be perfect, or it doesn't count.* This is the invisible script that runs the lives of so many depleted women. It is the belief that our value is tied to our output, and that our output must be flawless to keep us safe from judgment. We are performing an identity when we bake those cupcakes. We are trying to prove that we have it all together, that we aren't "glitching," and that we are worthy of the space we take up in the world.

## The Perfectionism Paradox

To understand why a woman who manages million-dollar budgets can be brought to her knees by a batch of frosting, we have to look at the difference between **Healthy Striving** and **Perfectionism**.

In the early 20th century, psychologists began to notice a specific pattern in high-achieving individuals. Alfred Adler, one of the founders of individual psychology, argued that everyone has an innate "striving for superiority." In its healthy form, this is what drives us to learn, grow, and improve our lives. It's the desire to do a good job because it feels good.

But perfectionism is something different. It isn't about self-improvement; it's about **Self-Protection**.

Perfectionism is a defensive shield we carry to prevent people from seeing our flaws. We believe that if we look, live, and work perfectly, we can avoid or minimize the painful feelings of shame, judgment, and blame. For the depleted woman, perfectionism is the ultimate "Guardian" strategy. If The Librarian can keep every file perfectly alphabetized and every "ocean breeze" cupcake perfectly frosted, then maybe, just maybe, no one will notice that she is actually hanging by a thread.

The paradox is that perfectionism actually makes us more vulnerable. Because the standard is unattainable, we live in a constant state of perceived failure. Every lumpy cupcake is a crack in the shield, not just a kitchen mishap. And when the shield cracks, the adrenaline floods back in, the stress cycle reopens, and we find ourselves right back in survival mode.

# The Roots of the "Good Girl" Programming

Most perfectionism isn't born in the boardroom or the kitchen; it's born in the classroom and the childhood home. This is what Dr. Aris calls "The Good Girl Programming."

Think back to your early school years. For many women, the path to safety and praise was paved with "A" grades, quiet hands, and a helpful attitude. We were socialized to be "little helpers" and "pleasers." While boys were often encouraged to take risks, get dirty, and break things, girls were frequently rewarded for being "correct."

This programming creates a deep neurological association: **Approval = Safety.**

If you are "good," people like you. If people like you, you are part of the "tribe." And as societal standards for women shift, you can challenge these expectations to feel more in control and confident.

By the time Sarah reached adulthood, this programming had evolved into a sophisticated internal system. She didn't just want to do her job; she wanted to be the *best* at her job, so her boss would never be disappointed. She didn't just want to be a mom; she wanted to be the mom who never snapped, never forgot a theme day, and always had the right shade of frosting. She was "Fawning" on a grand scale, using perfectionism to manage the emotions of everyone around her.

# People-Pleasing as a Fawn Response

In Chapter 2, we looked at Fight, Flight, and Freeze. But there is a fourth response that is particularly common among depleted women: **Fawning**.

Fawning is a survival strategy in which you attempt to avoid conflict or "threats" by becoming useful and agreeable, and by anticipating what others need. It is the "people-pleasing" response taken to a biological extreme. When you are in a Fawn response, you lose the ability to say "no" because saying "no" feels like a threat to your connection with the tribe.

Sarah's "Ocean Breeze" cupcakes were a Fan response. She didn't actually have the time or energy to bake from scratch. She was already working overtime to cover for a colleague, and Leo's soccer schedule was draining her battery. But when the PTA coordinator sent out the sign-up sheet, Sarah's brain perceived the empty slot as a "threat." She worried that if she didn't sign up, people would think she was "checked out" or "not a team player."

She said "yes" to protect her social standing, but her body paid the price. Her Fawn response forced her into the kitchen at midnight, where her exhausted Librarian couldn't follow a simple recipe. This led to the grainy cement frosting and eventual breakdown.

## The Cost of "Good Enough" Feeling Dangerous

If you tell a perfectionist to "just lower the bar," they will often look at you with genuine fear. To a regulated person, a 70% effort is a smart way to manage time. To a depleted woman in survival mode, 70% feels like a cliff's edge.

This is because your nervous system has associated "less than perfect" with "danger." When Sarah looked at her lumpy cupcakes, her Guardian didn't see food; it saw a social catastrophe. It triggered the same alarm system as the rolling car in the driveway. Her brain was screaming, *If you take these to school, people will judge you. If they judge you, you aren't safe. You have to fix this!*

This is why we can't "just relax" about the messy house or the imperfect email. Our biology has hijacked our standards. We aren't being "picky"; we are being protective. We are trying to prevent the "shame storm" that our brain predicts will happen if we show up as our messy, tired, authentic selves.

## Contrast the Perfectionist vs. the Enoughist

To see the way out, we have to look at two different approaches to the same reality. Let's look at two versions of Sarah Miller facing a common scenario: a Saturday morning where the house is a mess and guests are coming over for a casual lunch.

- **Perfectionist Sarah** wakes up with a racing heart. She sees the dust on the coffee table and feels a surge of cortisol. She spends three hours frantically cleaning, snapping at Mark for not helping "correctly," and hiding piles of mail in the oven. By the time the guests arrive, she is physically exhausted and emotionally "brittle." She spends the entire lunch monitoring the room. She checks for crumbs, worries if the salad is too wilted, and plays the role of the "Gracious Hostess." She is "there," but she isn't present. When the guests leave, she collapses into a "shutdown" state, unable to move for the rest of the day.

- **Enoughist Sarah** (the version Sarah is working to become) wakes up and sees the mess. She feels the initial spike of stress, but she uses a Physiological Sigh to reset. She looks at the coffee table and asks herself, *Does the dust prevent us from having a good conversation?* She decides to spend twenty minutes tidying the main areas and leaves the mail on the counter. She tells the guests, upon their arrival, "Sorry about the mess, it's been a wild week." She eats the lunch, laughs at a story, and actually hears what her friends are saying. When they leave, she still has 40% of her battery left. She hasn't "won" the morning, but she has *lived* it.

The difference isn't in the house; it's in the **Enough Filter**. The Perfectionist is trying to prevent judgment. The Enoughist is prioritizing connection and energy.

# Insight into Excellence Without Perfection

The turning point for Sarah came when she realized that her perfectionism was actually preventing her from being excellent.

Excellence is about the quality of the work. Perfectionism is about the quality of the *image*. When Sarah was obsessed with the frosting, she was so stressed that she forgot to put the eggs in the first batch of batter. Trying to be perfect made her less efficient, more prone to mistakes, and completely miserable.

Dr. Aris often explains that "Excellence" is a sustainable value, while "Perfection" is a finite resource. You can be excellent for a lifetime. You can only be perfect for a few minutes before the reality of being a human being catches up with you.

When you aim for "Enough," you are actually giving excellence room to grow. Because you aren't wasting 50% of your energy on "performing" calm, you have that 50% available actually to be calm. You are no longer a "Functional Freeze" woman; you are a woman who can respond to the world with her full intelligence.

# The "Enough Filter" has Three Questions to Reclaim Your Life.

To dismantle the perfectionism trap, you need a practical tool to use in the moment when the "Good Girl" programming starts to scream. Sarah started using the **Enough Filter**: three questions she would ask herself before putting energy into any task.

## 1. What is the actual "Standard of Safety" here?

Is this a task where perfection actually matters (like a surgery or a legal document), or is this a "Plastic Plate" (like a bake sale or a clean floor)? If the world won't end if it's done at 70%, then 70% is the goal.

## 2. Who am I performing for right now?

Am I doing this because it brings me joy, or am I doing it because I'm afraid of what Graham will think? If the answer is "fear of judgment," it's a Fawn response. Acknowledge it, and permit yourself to disappoint that imaginary judge.

## 3. What is the "Cost of the Polish"?

Every extra 10% of "perfection" costs way more energy. Going from "good enough" to "perfect" takes more energy than the entire rest of the task combined. Is the "polish" on this project worth the "Mom Snap" that will happen tonight because you're too tired to handle a spilled juice box?

# Sarah Used The 70% Experiment.

After the midnight cupcake breakdown, Sarah decided to try an experiment. She called it "The Week of 70%." She committed to doing every non-essential task at a "C-grade" level on purpose.

She sent work emails with minor typos (and didn't send a follow-up apology). She let the kids wear slightly wrinkled clothes to school. She bought a pre-made rotisserie chicken for dinner three nights in a row.

The first two days were excruciating. Her Guardian was on high alert. Every time she left a dish in the sink, she felt a "ping" of anxiety in her chest. She felt like she was "losing her grip." But by Wednesday, something strange happened.

The anxiety started to fade. She noticed that no one was calling her out. Her boss didn't mention the typos. Her kids didn't care about the chicken. The "shame storm" she had been running from for thirty-nine years never arrived.

She discovered that most of the pressure she felt came from **Internalized Expectations**. She had been holding herself to a standard that no one else was actually demanding. By doing things at 70%, she finally saw the truth: she was allowed to be a person, not a performance.

## A Historical Perspective of the "Ideal Woman" as a Moving Target

It's helpful to remember that the "standard" we are killing ourselves to meet is a relatively recent invention.

In the 18th century, a "good woman" was defined by her physical labor and her ability to survive. In the 1950s, she was defined by her domestic curation. Today, the "Ideal Woman" is expected to be a high-powered professional, a "present" and "gentle" parent, a fitness enthusiast, and a domestic goddess, all while maintaining a "minimalist" and "clean" aesthetic.

We are living in the first era of history in which women are expected to master every area of life at the same time. The "bar" isn't high; it's non-existent. It is a horizon line that moves further away the faster you run toward it.

When you realize that the "Ideal" is a cultural construct designed to keep you busy and consuming, it becomes easier to stop chasing it. You can start defining "Enough" based on your own values, energy, and soul.

## Identity Erosion Questions: Are You You Without the Shield?

One of the scariest parts of letting go of perfectionism is the question of identity. For Sarah, being "The One Who Has It All Together" was who she was. She was the "Human Sticky Note." If she stopped being perfect, who would she be?

This is Identity Erosion, which happens when we spend too much time in survival mode. We become our roles. We become our "plates." We forget that there is a woman underneath the performance who has her own desires, her own humor, and her own needs.

The "enough" practice is like an excavation. By clearing away the unnecessary "polish" of perfectionism, you start to see the "you" that was buried under the demands. You find that you are actually funnier when you aren't exhausted. You find that you are more creative when you aren't terrified of making a mistake. You find that you are *more* than enough, simply because you are imperfect.

## Sarah Hopes for the Safety of Being Seen

The best part of Sarah's "70% Experiment" wasn't the extra sleep; it was the change in her relationships.

When Sarah was "perfect," she was hard to talk to. She was so busy performing that she didn't have room for other people's messiness. Mark felt like he was always "doing it wrong" because his standards didn't match hers, which were impossible. Her kids felt the "vibration" of her stress and became more anxious themselves.

But when Sarah started showing up as "Enough," the house relaxed. When she admitted she was tired, Mark felt like he might be, too. When she laughed at the lumpy cupcakes, Leo realized that it was okay to make mistakes.

By letting her shield drop, Sarah was inviting her family to do the same. She was creating a "Culture of Enough" in her home. She was proving that love isn't earned through a flawless performance; it exists in the messy, lumpy, grainy reality of being human.

## Today, Do One Thing at 70% on Purpose.

Today, I want you to pick one low-stakes task and do it "badly" on purpose. - Send an email without proofreading it three times.

- Fold the towels "the wrong way" and put them in the closet.

- Leave the bed unmade.

- Buy the store-bought cookies and put them on a plate without pretending you made them.

As you do it, pay close attention to your body. You will likely feel a "surge" of discomfort. Your Guardian will tell you that you are being lazy or that people will notice.

**Sit with that discomfort.** Don't rush to fix it. Don't apologize for it. Just observe the feeling. Tell your nervous system: *"I am doing this at 70% on purpose. We are safe. The world is not ending."*

Each time you do this, you are "rewiring" your brain. You are building the muscle of the "Enoughist." You are teaching your body that you don't have to be perfect to be protected.

# The Transformation of Sarah Miller

Remember those "ocean breeze" cupcakes?

A week after the disaster, there was another event, a small "thank you" lunch for the teachers. Usually, Sarah would have spent three hours on a gourmet pasta salad.

Instead, she walked into the grocery store, bought two large bags of high-quality chips, and a tub of pre-made dip. She put them in a nice bowl and walked into the school.

She felt a tiny twinge of the "Good Girl" guilt as she saw another mom arrive with a homemade quiche. But then, she saw the teachers. They were tired. They were hungry. They fell upon the chips and dip with pure joy. One of them said, "Oh my god, I haven't had these chips in forever. This is exactly what I needed."

Sarah stood there, holding her empty bowl, and felt a wave of genuine calm. She hadn't performed. She hadn't stressed. She had provided exactly "enough," and it was perfect.

She realized that the "magic" wasn't in the pasta salad. It was in her being able to stand there, talk to the teachers, and feel like she belonged in the room without having to "earn" her seat.

## The Cliffhanger, Uh-Oh, The Barrier of "No"

Sarah was finding her way to "Enough." She was clearing the stress from her body and lowering the bar for her own performance. She felt lighter than she had in years.

But then, she hit the final, most difficult wall.

It happened on a Thursday afternoon. Her phone buzzed with a text from her sister: *"Hey, can you host Mom's birthday dinner this Sunday? I'm totally swamped, and you're so much better at that stuff anyway!"*

Sarah's heart didn't just "ping," it hammered. Her "Enough Filter" told her the answer was a clear "no." She had no energy left for a dinner party. Her nervous system was begging for a quiet Sunday.

But as she stared at the screen, her thumb hovered over the keyboard. She knew what she *wanted* to say, but she felt a physical wave of nausea at the thought of actually saying it. She realized that it was one thing to do her *own* tasks at 70%, but another entirely to tell someone else "no."

She had learned to lower the bar, but she hadn't yet learned how to build a fence. She realized that all the "calm" in the world wouldn't stay if she kept letting other people's demands walk right through her front door. She was ready to say no, but she was terrified of the "guilt hangover" that she knew would follow.

She realized that the final step to a calmer life wasn't just about what she did, it was about what she refused to do. And she had no idea if she was brave enough to hold the line.

# Chapter Seven

# Saying No Without the Guilt Hangover

## Boundaries That Actually Hold

If you walk into the kitchen of the Miller house on a Sunday afternoon today, you will find a room that feels surprisingly still. There is a stack of mail on the counter, but it isn't vibrating with urgency. The refrigerator is stocked, but not overflowing. Most notably, Sarah Miller is sitting at the kitchen island, a book in hand, a cup of tea in hand, and a look of quiet focus. The house is not "perfect," but it is calm.

However, if you had stood in this exact spot just four months ago, the air would have felt thick with a different kind of energy. You would have seen Sarah standing where she is now, but her body would have been rigid, her eyes darting between a bubbling pot of pasta and the glowing screen of her phone. On that specific Sunday, the kitchen was a stage for a silent, desperate performance. Her sister had texted asking her to host their mother's birthday dinner. Sarah's internal battery was at 4%. Her jaw was already locked in that familiar "survival mode" grip. Every fiber of her being was screaming *no*, but her thumbs were typing *Yes, of course! What time works for everyone?*

She wasn't saying yes because she wanted to host. She was saying yes because she didn't have a fence. She had spent thirty-nine years living in a house with no front door; anyone could walk in, rearrange the furniture, and leave their trash on the floor, and Sarah would apologize for the mess. She had learned to lower her own standards, but she hadn't yet learned that she was allowed to stop other people from setting them for her. She was terrified that if she said the word *no*, the "Good Girl" image she had built would shatter, leaving her alone, judged, and cast out from the tribe.

## The Willpower Myth

We often talk about boundaries as if they are a matter of "willpower" or "bravery." We tell ourselves that if we were just stronger or more confident, we could stand up for ourselves. But the reality of the depleted woman is that boundaries are not a personality trait. They are a matter of **capacity**.

In the mid-20th century, researchers began studying a phenomenon known as "ego depletion." The theory suggested that willpower is a finite resource, like a battery. Every time you make a decision, resist a temptation, or force yourself to be pleasant when you are angry, you use up a bit of that battery. By the time a woman like Sarah reaches 5:00 p.m. after a day of "spinning plates," her willpower battery is beyond low; it's dead.

When your sister asks you to host a dinner, and you are already in "Functional Freeze," you don't have the neurological resources to handle the conflict of a "no." Saying "yes" is actually the path of least resistance for a fried nervous system. It feels easier to do the work of a dinner party than to handle the "threat" of a disappointed family member.

Boundaries are essential for your well-being, not a test of character, which can help women feel empowered to prioritize their health.

# The Anatomy of a Boundary

To build a fence that actually holds, you have to recognize when your boundaries are being distorted. Understanding what you are protecting helps you identify where your limits are being crossed. For the depleted woman, three specific types of lines-Time Boundaries, Energy Boundaries, and Identity Boundaries-are often blurred or broken, making it harder to maintain healthy limits.

**Time Boundaries** are the most visible. This is the fence around your calendar. It is the realization that your hours are a non-renewable resource. When someone asks for "just a quick call" or "a small favor," they are asking for a piece of your life that you will never get back.

**Energy Boundaries** are more subtle. These are about protecting your "vibration." You might have the *time* to go to a loud, chaotic birthday party, but do you have the *energy*? If you go, will you be so "touched out" that you can't sleep that night? An energy boundary is the right to say, "I have the time, but I don't have the bandwidth."

**Identity Boundaries** are the deepest. These protect your right to be a person, not a utility. When Sarah's sister said, "You're so much better at that stuff anyway," she was crossing an identity boundary. She was defining Sarah by her usefulness. An identity boundary is the internal fence that says, *I am not a 'Human Sticky Note." I am a person who is allowed to be tired and* to have needs that exist independently of how I can serve others.

# The Backlash Effect

One of the reasons Sarah found it so hard to say no was a very real social phenomenon called the **Backlash Effect**. Research has consistently shown that when women act with agency, meaning they are assertive, direct, and protective of their own interests, they are often penalized in ways men are not.

When a man says "no" to a project, he is often seen as "decisive" or "focused." When a woman says "no," she is frequently perceived as "uncooperative," "cold," or "not a team player." This is a documented cultural bias, not just in Sarah's head.

This creates a "Guilt Loop." Your biology tells you to protect yourself, but your social brain knows that doing so might come at a cost. You are caught between the "Mom Snap" (internal cost) and "Social Rejection" (external cost). For years, Sarah had chosen the internal cost. She would rather burn herself out than risk someone thinking she was "difficult."

Dr. Aris emphasizes that if the people in your life only love you when you say "yes," they don't truly love you. Recognizing this can be a first step toward setting boundaries. Practical strategies include practicing small 'no's in safe environments and reminding yourself that boundaries protect your well-being, not your worth. This empowers you to act without guilt, even when social backlash feels intimidating.

## The Guilt Hangover

The most important insight Sarah gained during her journey was the realization that **guilt is not a sign that you did something wrong.**

In the language of the nervous system, the guilt you feel after saying "no" is actually a "Social Rejection Alarm." Because we are tribal animals, our brains perceive a disappointed sister or an annoyed boss as a threat to our safety. Your Guardian starts screaming: "Fix it!" *Make them happy! Apologize!*

This is the **Guilt Hangover**. It feels like a physical sickness, a pit in your stomach, a racing heart, a loop of "I should have just done it."

Sarah used to think that if she felt guilty, it meant her "no" was a mistake. She would say "no," feel the hangover for 10 minutes, and then immediately text back: *"Actually, I can make it work!" Forget what I said!*

She had to learn to treat the guilt hangover like a common cold. It's uncomfortable, it's annoying, but it isn't an emergency. It is just your old "Good Girl" programming clearing out of your system. If you can sit with the discomfort for seventy-two hours without "fixing" the situation, the alarm will eventually turn itself off. You have to be brave enough to feel bad while doing the right thing.

## The Three-Part Boundary Framework

To help her Librarian stay in the chair during high-stakes moments, Sarah started using a three-part script. This took the "willpower" out of the equation and gave her a logical structure to follow when her heart was hammering.

1. **Acknowledge and Validate:** Start by showing you heard the request. This lowers the other person's defenses and proves you aren't being "mean." *(e.g., "I know Mom's birthday is really important, and I love that you want to make it special.")*

2. **State the Boundary (Without Over-Explaining):** This is the hard part. You must state the "no" clearly, without offering excuses. Excuses are handles that people can use to pull your fence down. *(e.g., "However, I don't have the capacity to host a dinner this weekend.")*

3. **The Optional Pivot:** If you want to be helpful without carrying the load, you can offer a different kind of support that doesn't cost your peace. *(e.g., "I'm happy to order the cake and have it delivered to your place, but I can't do the hosting.")*

When Sarah first used this script with her sister, she felt like she was jumping out of a plane without a parachute. She sent the text and then literally threw her phone across the couch so she wouldn't have to see the reply. She felt the "Guilt Hangover" immediately. She felt like a "bad sister." She felt like a "mess."

But three hours later, her sister replied, *"No worries!" I'll check with Mark's brother. Do you have the number for that cake place?*

The world didn't end. Her sister wasn't mad. The "shame storm" was only happening inside Sarah's head. By clearly stating her capacity, she gave her sister the chance to solve the problem differently. She had stopped being the "Safety Net" and started being a "Partner."

## The 72-Hour Rule

A helpful tool Dr. Aris taught Sarah was the **72-Hour Rule**. When you set a new boundary with someone who is used to your "unlimited yes," there is often a period of friction. They might push back, get quiet, or try to "guilt" you back into your old role.

The 72-Hour Rule states that you are not allowed to "fix," apologize for, or change your boundary for three full days. You have to let the "vibration" of the "no" settle.

During those seventy-two hours, your job is to use your "Cycle Completers." Shake, breathe, cry, or talk to a friend who understands boundaries. You are "weathering the storm." Usually, by the end of the third day, the other person has gotten used to the change, and your own nervous system has realized that you are still alive despite the "no."

## Situations Where You Are Allowed to Say No

To help Sarah realize how much space she was allowed to take up, she created a "Permission List" and kept it in her bedside drawer. It was a reminder that her "no" wasn't a crime; it was healthcare.

- **Social events where the primary goal is "performing"**: If you are going just so people won't ask why you aren't there, you are allowed to stay home.

- **Unasked-for advice or "help" that feels like a chore**: You don't have to accept every "gift" that comes with a string attached.

- **Sex when you are "touched out"**: Your body belongs to you, even in a marriage. If your nervous system is on high alert, intimacy can feel like one more demand. You are allowed to prioritize your physical safety and comfort.

- **"Quick" work tasks that happen after hours**: You are not a 24-hour emergency room unless you are literally a doctor on call.

- **Taking on the emotional labor of a friend's crisis when you are empty**: You can love someone and still not have the energy to be their therapist today.

## Sarah's Check-In: The Sunday Shift

Which brings us back to that Sunday afternoon in the kitchen.

Sarah's sister did end up hosting the dinner. Sarah arrived with the cake she had ordered, stayed for two hours, and then told the family, "This was lovely, but I'm going to head out now so I can get a jump on the week."

In the old days, Sarah would have stayed until 10:00 p.m., washing the dishes at her sister's house to "make up" for not hosting. She would have arrived home exhausted and resentful.

Today, she arrived home at 7:30 p.m. She had time to take a long shower, read her book, and actually talk to Mark without snapping. She felt a tiny, lingering spark of guilt; the "Good Girl" ghost still haunts the hallways, but she recognized it for what it was. It was just a feeling, not a fact.

She had learned that a boundary isn't a wall that keeps people out; it's a gate that lets her stay in. By saying "no" to the dinner, she had said "yes" to herself. She had protected her Window of Tolerance so she could show up on Monday as a whole person rather than feel like she was falling apart.

# The Bridge to the System

Sarah was feeling the power of her "no." She was regulating her nervous system, lowering her standards, and holding her fences. She felt like she was finally winning the internal war.

But as she sat in her quiet kitchen, she looked around and realized something frustrating. Even though *she* felt better, the *house* was still a mess of daily chores. She had said "no" to her sister, but she still hadn't figured out how to get Mark to notice the milk was low. She had protected her energy, but she was still the only one who knew where the soccer cleats were.

She realized that boundaries could protect her from *new* work, but they couldn't fix the *existing* load that was already sitting on her shoulders. She had the fence, but she was still the only one doing the farming.

She saw clearly that focusing only on herself goes only so far. To truly find a life she didn't want to escape, she had to move beyond "mindset" and "boundaries." She had to look at the actual systems of her life. She needed to figure out how to stop being the "Manager" and start building a household that functioned like a team, even when she wasn't the one holding the whistle.

She was ready to stop just "coping" with the load. She was ready to move it.

# Chapter Eight

# Redistributing the Load

## Systems That Work With Your Life, Not Against It

I f you were to hover like a bird over a typical suburban street at 7:15 on a Tuesday morning, you would see the coordinated routine of morning logistics. From this height, the individual faces disappear, replaced by the rhythmic opening and closing of garage doors. You would see the flickering brake lights of SUVs idling in driveways. You would see small figures in backpacks being ushered into backseats like precious cargo being loaded onto transport ships.

From above, it looks like a well-oiled machine. But if you zoomed in closer, you would see the frantic "vibration" of the woman behind the wheel. You would see the silent lip-syncing of grocery lists, the white-knuckled grip on steering wheels, and the quick, desperate checks of cell phones at red lights. This is the "Organization Trap" in motion. Many women feel overwhelmed trying to solve an impossible life with better organization, hoping the right system will ease the burden.

But on one particular Tuesday, Sarah Miller broke the pattern. While the garage doors on her street rose in unison, Sarah remained at her kitchen island. She wasn't moving. She wasn't packing a lunch. She was looking at a single piece of paper. For ten years, Sarah had been the "Human Sticky Note," the person who tracked every single need in the house. She had tried every productivity hack in the book. She concluded that you cannot "optimize" your way out of carrying too much. But her realization opened a new path: change is possible, and systems can bring relief.

Sarah realized that her problem wasn't a lack of discipline; it was a lack of infrastructure. She was trying to run a complex corporation using only her own memory and a few scattered Post-it notes. To find true calm, she had to move from being the person who *did* the work to the person who *designed the system* that did the work. She had to shift from individual effort to a more effective way of sharing the work.

## The Organization Trap

We have been sold a very specific fantasy: that the secret to a calm life is a perfectly organized pantry. We are told that if we buy enough clear acrylic containers and label them in cursive, our internal chaos will vanish. This is the Organization Trap. It treats the symptoms of depletion while ignoring the cause.

Organization is about *how* you carry the load. Redistribution is about *how much* you carry.

When Sarah first started, she spent a lot of time trying to "optimize" her stress. She created a more efficient way to track school theme days. She bought a better planner to manage the meal prep. She was becoming a world-class manager of her own exhaustion. But the load itself stayed the same size. She was still the only person noticing, tracking, and executing.

A system works when a task no longer requires your "noticing" to get done. If you have to remind your partner to take out the trash, you are still carrying the mental load. If the system is "The trash goes out every Tuesday night, and Mark owns the entire process from noticing the bag is full to putting a new liner in," then the task has been successfully moved out of your brain. This shift in ownership can empower you to feel more in control and less overwhelmed.

## The Family Load Audit

To move a load, you first have to see its true dimensions. Most women carry their work in a blurry cloud of "everything." To redistribute it, we have to turn that cloud into a map.

Sarah and Mark sat down for what they called the 'Family Load Audit' to identify and understand their household responsibilities. They didn't do it in the middle of a fight, nor when exhaustion was high. They chose a calm Saturday morning after coffee to honestly assess every recurring task, making the invisible visible to facilitate real change.

- **The Daily Maintenance**: Dishes, laundry, pet feeding, and mail.

- **The Logistical Puzzles**: School forms, doctor appointments, car maintenance, and bills.

- **The Emotional/Social Work**: Birthday gifts, checking on parents, managing kid friendships.

- **The Anticipatory Scanning**: Noticing we are low on soap, planning next season's clothes, tracking the weather for outdoor events.

When Sarah laid these out on the table, Mark was genuinely shocked. He saw himself as a "helpful" husband. He did the dishes when asked. He mowed the lawn. But when he saw the list, he realized he was a "Doer" in a house where Sarah was the only "Manager." He was waiting for instructions, while Sarah was drowning in the labor of *giving* those instructions.

The point of the audit isn't to blame; it's to show the "Manager vs. Doer" gap. If you are the only one who knows the dentist's name, you are the Manager of health. If you are the only one who knows which day is library day, you are the Manager of Education. To redistribute the load, you have to hand over the **Full Ownership** of the category, not just the individual tasks.

# Delegate, Diminish, Default

The 3 D's-Delegate, Diminish, Default-are practical steps to help you lessen mental clutter. Using these strategies can stop the 'vibration' in your brain by removing the need to constantly think about household tasks.

## 1. Delegate (Full Ownership)

Delegation only works if you hand over the 'CPE': Conception, Planning, and Execution. If Sarah asks Mark to 'help with dinner,' she still retains the mental load of deciding what to cook and gathering ingredients. Full ownership means entrusting him with all aspects of the task, from start to finish.

To Delegate, Sarah handed Mark the "Tuesday/Thursday Dinner Plate." On those days, Mark was responsible for deciding the menu, checking the pantry, and cooking the meal. Sarah was not allowed to offer suggestions or "save" him if he forgot an ingredient. She had to be brave enough to let the system work, even if it meant eating cereal for dinner once or twice while Mark learned the ropes.

## 2. Diminish (Lower Frequency/Standard)

This is where you look at tasks that don't need to be done as often or as perfectly as you think. Sarah realized she was washing the bedsheets every single week because she thought that's what "good moms" did. She diminished the frequency to every two weeks. She saved fifty-two loads of laundry a year with one decision.

Ask yourself: What am I doing out of habit that doesn't actually add value to my life? If you stop folding the kids' pajamas and toss them in a drawer, what is the actual cost? Usually, the cost is zero, but the energy saved is significant.

## 3. Default (Automate Decisions)

Decision fatigue is a main cause of depletion. Every time you have to choose what's for dinner or which detergent to buy, you use a "sip" of your mental energy.

Sarah put as many decisions as possible in "Default" mode.

- **The Uniform**: She bought five identical pairs of work pants and seven identical shirts. She never had to choose an outfit again.

- **The Subscription**: Every household staple (toilet paper, soap, dog food) was put on a recurring Amazon subscription. She stopped "noticing" when things were low because the box arrived.

- **The Tuesday Taco**: Every Tuesday was Taco Night—no planning, no debate, no "what do you want for dinner?" loop.

# The Problem of "Gatekeeping"

The biggest obstacle to redistributing the load isn't usually the partner. It's the woman's own nervous system. This is called **Maternal Gatekeeping** or "Managerial Control."

When Sarah handed the "Laundry Plate" to Mark, she found herself hovering. She saw him folding the shirts "the wrong way." She saw him mixing white and colored paint. Her Guardian started screaming that the clothes would be ruined, that the kids would look messy, and that she should "do it herself because it's faster."

This is a trap. When you step in to "correct" a task, you are taking ownership back. You are telling your partner that they are a volunteer and you are the boss. You are also telling your own brain that it isn't safe to stop tracking the laundry.

To make systems work, you have to accept a **"Close Enough" Standard**. If the shirts are wrinkled but clean, that is a success. If the kids eat hot dogs for the third night in a row, but you have to read a book, that is a win. You have to value your peace more than you value the "correct" way of folding a towel.

## The Family Dashboard

Sarah and Mark realized they needed a "Source of Truth" that wasn't Sarah's brain. They created a **Family Dashboard** in the kitchen. It wasn't a fancy digital screen; it was a simple whiteboard with three sections:

1. **The Week at a Glance**: Only the "non-negotiables" (soccer, meetings, birthdays).

2. **The "Out Of" List**: Anyone who uses the last of something must write it down. If it's not on the list, it doesn't get bought.

3. **The Owner of the Day**: Who is the "Primary Parent" on call? Who is the "Dinner Owner"?

This dashboard moved the information from the internal (Sarah's head) to the external (the wall). When Leo needed to know if he had soccer, he stopped asking Sarah; he looked at the board. When Mark saw they were out of eggs, he didn't tell Sarah; he wrote it on the list.

The "vibration" in Sarah's head began to quiet. She was no longer the "Router" for all information. She was just a person in the house.

## The 15-Minute Weekly Reset

Systems require maintenance, but they shouldn't require a marathon. Sarah and Mark started a "Sunday Reset." For exactly fifteen minutes, they sat down and looked at the week ahead.

- "Who is driving on Thursday?"

- "Do we need a gift for that party?"

- "What is the one big stressor we can see coming?"

By spending 15 minutes on "Anticipatory Labor" together, they avoided 5 hours of "Crisis Management" later in the week. It turned them from two people reacting to chaos into a team with a plan.

## Systems for Single Mothers

If you are reading this and you don't have a partner to delegate to, the concept of "redistribution" can feel like a cruel joke. But for single mothers, systems are even more essential because there is no "backup" battery.

For Sarah's friend Elena, a single mom of two, redistribution meant looking outside the home.

- **The "Village" Swap**: Elena teamed up with another single mom. Every Wednesday, Elena took all four kids so the other mom could work or rest. Every Thursday, they swapped. They "delegated" childcare to each other.

- **Extreme Defaulting**: Elena reduced her household to the bare essentials. She used paper plates two nights a week to eliminate the "Dish Plate." She moved all the kids' clothes to a "basket system" where nothing was folded. It was just sorted by type.

- **The "No-Notice" Zone**: Elena identified the tasks that caused her the most mental "noise" and automated them ruthlessly. She set up auto-pay for every single bill, even the small ones, so she never had to "remember" a due date again.

For the solo parent, the goal is to diminish the load to fit the capacity of one human being. It is about the radical rejection of "shoulds." If you are a single mom, you do not "should" have a perfectly organized pantry. You "should" have a regulated nervous system.

## When the System Breaks

No system is perfect. Mark will forget a doctor's appointment. The Amazon subscription will send the wrong soap. The "Tuesday Taco" will eventually get boring.

When the system breaks, the depleted woman's instinct is to snatch the plate back and say, "See? I knew I had to do it myself!"

This is the moment of truth. Instead of taking the plate back, you must troubleshoot **the System, not the Person.**

- Instead of "You forgot the appointment," try "The calendar alert didn't work. How can we make sure the system notifies you better next time?"

- Instead of "I'll just do the grocery list from now on," try "We missed the eggs. Let's move the list to a place where it's easier to see."

By keeping the focus on the structure, you protect the relationship and your own progress. You are teaching your family that the "Manager" role is closed for business.

# The "Cleat" Victory

A month after starting the Dashboard, Sarah had a moment that showed the system was holding.

Leo came into the kitchen on a Wednesday afternoon. "Mom, my cleats are really tight. I need bigger ones for the game tomorrow."

In the old days, Sarah's heart would have spiked. She would have opened her phone, searched for a store, checked her calendar, and felt the familiar surge of "Anticipatory Panic."

Instead, Sarah took a sip of her tea. She didn't even look up from her book. "Mark is the Owner of Soccer this month, Leo. Go talk to him."

She heard the footsteps move toward the living room. She heard the muffled conversation between father and son. She heard the jingling of car keys as Mark said, "Alright, let's go find some shoes."

Sarah sat perfectly still. Her Librarian wanted to jump up and ask Mark where the "good" sporting goods store was. Her Guardian wanted to make sure they didn't spend too much money. But Sarah stayed in her chair. She took a Physiological Sigh. She realized that for the first time in a decade, a problem was being solved in her house, and she wasn't the one solving it.

She wasn't "lazy." She was unnecessary. And in that moment, "unnecessary" felt like the most beautiful word in the English language.

# A Historical Example of the Efficiency of the Shakers

The struggle to balance labor and life is not new. In the 1800s, the religious community known as the Shakers became famous for their incredible efficiency and calm. They were the inventors of the circular saw, the clothespin, and the flat broom. They lived in large communal houses where the labor was divided with mathematical precision.

The Shakers didn't work harder than their neighbors; they worked **smarter**. They believed that "order is heaven's first law." They created systems for everything, from how the laundry was moved through the house to how the seeds were sorted for the garden. They were obsessed with "labor-saving devices" because they believed that the less time you spent on the "grind" of survival, the more time you had for the spirit.

Their furniture reflected this philosophy. Shaker chairs were designed to hang from wall pegs when not in use, making it easier to clean the floors. Everything had a "Default" place. Every person had a "Delegated" ownership.

The lesson of the Shakers is that calm is not a lucky accident. It is a byproduct of design. They didn't find peace by trying to be "better" people; they found peace by building a world that made it easy to be calm.

In our modern world, we build our own mini-societies. We can choose to live in a "Manual Labor" household where the woman handles everything, or we can build a "Shaker" household where the systems carry the weight.

## The Bridge to the Soul

Sarah Miller had successfully redistributed the load. Her nervous system was regulated. Her boundaries were holding. Her house was running on a system that didn't require her to be a "Human Sticky Note."

She had achieved the "Calm" that the book promised. She was no longer depleted.

But as the noise of chores and logistics faded, a new, quieter sound emerged. It was a question that Sarah hadn't had the "bandwidth" to ask for ten years.

Now that she wasn't "The Manager," who was she? Now that she wasn't defined by her "usefulness," what did she actually like? She realized that she had been so busy surviving the chaos that she had forgotten to live her own life. She had cleared the space, but now she had to figure out what to put in it.

She had found the calm, but now she needed to find herself. She was about to realize that the end of depletion is the presence of joy, not simply the absence of work. And for a woman who had been a "Manager" for a decade, joy was the most terrifying "system" of all to implement.

# Chapter Nine

# Finding Yourself Under All of It

## Identity, Joy, and the Woman You Were Before the Chaos

In 1941, a woman named Anna Mary Robertson Moses was facing a crisis of utility. To her neighbors in upstate New York, she was "Mother Moses," a woman who had spent her entire life in the relentless service of others. She had birthed ten children and buried five. She had spent decades churning butter, stitching clothes, and managing the brutal logistics of a farm. Her hands were gnarled by arthritis, and her body was a map of the labor required to keep a family alive in a demanding world.

When her husband died, and her children grew up, the "Manager" role she had occupied for 70 years suddenly vanished. The systems were gone. The plates had stopped spinning. Most people expected her to fade into the quiet gray of old age. But Anna Mary did something that confused everyone around her. She didn't want to "rest." She felt a strange, nagging pull toward the girl she had been, the one who painted "landscapes" with grape juice on old boards.

She picked up a brush. She began to paint scenes from the life she had lived: maple sugaring, wash days, and country fairs. She wasn't trying to be a "professional." She was a reluctant pioneer of her own joy. When a collector spotted her work in a local drugstore window, the world met "Grandma Moses." She became a global sensation not because she was a technical master, but because she represented something the modern world was starving for: a woman who had successfully excavated herself from the mountain of her own duties.

Anna Mary didn't start painting because she had "free time." She started because the absence of her roles left a void that only her true self could fill. When she finally sat down to paint, she wasn't returning to an old self; she was integrating everything she had learned into a new, lively expression of who she actually was. This shows that the "you" beneath the chaos is still there, waiting to be rediscovered, inspiring hope and a sense of possibility for women who feel lost.

## The Erosion of the Self

If you feel like you have "lost yourself" in the years since you took on the mental load of a family and a career, you are experiencing a biological and social process called **Identity Erosion**.

This is the quiet, creeping feeling that the person who used to love late-night movies, spicy food, or obscure history podcasts has been replaced by a "Manager" who only cares about the price of eggs and the timing of soccer practice. It happens because your brain is a survival machine. As we saw in the science of survival mode, when your system is constantly scanning for threats and managing logistics, it favors "utility" over "identity."

Identity is a luxury of the safe and the rested. When you are in survival mode, your brain treats "joy" or "hobbies" as non-essential data. It prunes away the neural pathways that lead to your personal interests to save energy for the "plates" you have to spin. Over time, the "you" who exists outside of your roles becomes a ghost. You look in the mirror, and you don't see a woman with a soul; you see a "Human Sticky Note" looking for a place to be useful.

## Matrescence and the Role Trap

In the 1970s, anthropologist Dana Raphael coined the term "matrescence" to describe the transition into motherhood. She argued that it is a developmental shift as massive as adolescence, affecting a woman's body, brain, and social standing. However, while we give teenagers grace as they "find themselves," we expect women undergoing matrescence to simply absorb their new role without losing an ounce of their old identity.

This creates the **Role Trap**. You are told you can "have it all," which you interpret as "being all things to all people." You become the project manager, the chef, the emotional thermostat, and the logistical coordinator. These roles are so loud and so demanding that they drown out your internal voice.

Sarah Miller felt this erosion deeply. One Saturday, Mark asked her, "What do you want to do for your birthday this year?"

Sarah opened her mouth to answer, and realized with a jolt of horror that she had no idea. She no longer had a favorite restaurant. She didn't know what kind of music she liked to listen to when the kids weren't in the car. She had spent a decade making decisions based on what would cause the least amount of friction for everyone else. Her own desires had become a "dead zone" on her internal map. She had successfully implemented the systems we discussed in Chapter 8. She had the calm, but she was standing in that calm like a stranger in her own house.

## The Excavation Process

Finding yourself isn't about "going back" to the person you were before the chaos. Instead, focus on practical steps to merge the woman who manages crises with the woman who feels joy. Start small, schedule time for activities that bring you happiness, and gradually build this integration into your routine.

This is an excavation. You are digging through the layers of "shoulds," "musts," and "Managerial duties" to find the artifacts of your own spirit. This isn't a quick fix; it's a slow, intentional process that requires patience and compassion, helping women feel supported rather than overwhelmed as they reclaim their identity.

## 1. The Joy Audit

We often think of joy as a reward for hard work. We tell ourselves, "If I get the house clean and the emails sent, then I can do something fun." But as a depleted woman, you will never reach the end of the work. Joy must be a Restorative Tool-small moments of pleasure that restore your spirit and remind you of your worth, empowering you to reclaim your happiness.

Look back at your life before the "Manager" took over. What were the things you did that had no "utility"? - Did you like the smell of oil paints? - Did you find peace in digging in the dirt? - Did you use to stay up late reading about the Tudor dynasty? - Did you love the feeling of running until your lungs burned?

Sarah remembered how much she loved "making things with her hands" that weren't school lunches. She remembered a pottery class she took in her twenties. She remembered the specific, cold weight of the clay. She saw that for ten years, the only thing her hands had "made" was order out of chaos.

## 2. Identifying the "Identity Leaks."

Just as we looked for "leaks" in your energy bucket, we have to look for leaks in your identity. These are the places where you are performing a role that you no longer believe in.

Are you still hosting that book club even though you hate the books? Are you still the "one who always brings the homemade cookies" because you're afraid of what will happen if you bring the store-bought ones? Every time you perform a role out of habit rather than heart, you are burying your true self a little deeper.

## 3. Protecting the "Un-Managed" Hour

The most radical thing a woman can do is to have entirely unmanaged time. This is a time when you are not a mother, a wife, or an employee. You are just a biological being in the world.

For Sarah, this meant implementing the "Saturday Morning Solo." For two hours every Saturday, Mark was the "Owner of the House." Sarah would leave. Sometimes she went to a coffee shop. Sometimes she just sat in the library. Most importantly, she didn't use this time for "errands." If she caught herself thinking about the grocery list, she would complete a Physiological Sigh and return to her book. She was practicing being a person who didn't have to produce anything.

# Joy Is Not a Luxury

There is a neurological reason why finding yourself is essential for long-term calm. When you do things that bring you "flow," that state of being so absorbed in something that time disappears, your brain releases a mix of dopamine, serotonin, and endorphins.

This is more than just "feeling good." These chemicals act as a biological buffer against stress. A woman who connects with her own joy is more resilient. When the "plates" start to wobble, she has an internal anchor that keeps her from being swept away by the panic. She knows that even if the "Manager" fails, the "Person" is still okay.

Dr. Aris often explains that a nervous system that is only used for "threat detection" and "logistics" becomes brittle. It loses its elasticity. Joy is the lubricant that keeps your nervous system flexible. It expands your Window of Tolerance. When you have something in your life that is "just for you," you aren't just having fun; you are doing vital maintenance on your ability to stay calm.

# Reclaiming Your Name

In the 19th century, it was common for women to be referred to in print as "Mrs. John Smith." Their very name was absorbed into their husband's identity. While we don't do that as often today, many women experience a "Mental Mrs. John Smith" effect. You become "Leo's Mom" or "Mark's Wife" or "The PM on the Smith Account."

Reclaiming your identity starts with reclaiming your name. This includes the word itself and the **authority** of your own preferences.

One of the most powerful exercises Sarah did was the "Preference Practice." For one week, every time she was asked a preference question (What do you want for dinner? What movie should we watch? What color should we paint the hallway?), she was not allowed to say "I don't care" or "Whatever everyone else wants." She had to identify an actual preference and state it.

"I want Thai food." "I want to watch the documentary, not the cartoon." "I think the blue is too dark; I want the sage green."

At first, it felt selfish. Her Fawn response was screaming at her to be "easy" and "pleasant." But as the week went on, she felt a strange new sensation: **Solidarity**. She was becoming a solid object in the room rather than a ghost. She was teaching her family and herself that she had boundaries, tastes, and a soul.

# Sarah's Excavation

Sarah sat at her kitchen island, but for the first time in months, she wasn't looking at the Dashboard. She was looking at a small, slightly lopsided clay bowl she had made at a "drop-in" pottery studio the day before.

It wasn't perfect. It wasn't "useful." It was actually too small to hold much more than a few paperclips. But as she ran her thumb over the rough edge, she felt a spark of something she hadn't felt in a long time. It was the feeling of **agency**. She had created something that didn't solve a problem. She had spent two hours in a room where no one called her "Mom."

"That's a cool bowl," Mark said, leaning over her shoulder. "Did you make that?"

"I did," Sarah said. She didn't add, *It's just a little thing* or *I know it's messy.* She just let the statement sit there. "I liked the way the clay felt. I think I'm going to go back next Saturday."

Mark nodded. "Cool. I'll make sure the kids have their soccer stuff ready, so you don't have to worry about it."

A year ago, Sarah would have felt guilty for leaving. She would have spent the whole pottery class worrying if Mark would remember the water bottles. But because she had the systems in place, and because she had learned to complete the stress cycle, she could actually **be** in the studio. She was finding the woman she'd been before the chaos, and she realized this new version was even better. She was a woman who could manage a life *and* enjoy it.

## The Integration Checklist

How do you know if you are successfully excavating yourself? The **Internal Shift** matters more than how many hobbies you have.

- **The Absence of "Permission Seeking"**: You stop asking "Is it okay if I...?" and start stating "I am going to..."

- **The Return of Curiosity**: You find yourself wondering about things that have nothing to do with your to-do list. You want to know how a certain bird migrates or how a certain recipe works.

- **The "Guilt-Free" Hour**: You can sit for thirty minutes without doing anything "productive" and your heart doesn't race.

- **The Reclamation of Humor**: You find yourself making jokes again. Humor is one of the first things to go in survival mode, and one of the first things to return when you feel safe.

## The Resistance: "This Feels Selfish"

The depleted woman's final defense against finding herself is the "Selfishness" shield. You have been taught that a "good" woman is a sacrificial one. You worry that if you focus on your own joy, your family will suffer.

But look at the reality of the "Sacrificial Woman." Is she calm? Is she present? Is she a joy to be around? No. She is brittle, resentful, and exhausted. She is a "Human Sticky Note" that has lost its stick.

When you find yourself, you are giving your family a gift. You are showing your children that a woman's life is not a series of chores to be endured, but a life to be lived. You are showing your partner that you are a whole person, which allows them to be one too. Finding yourself isn't selfish; it is the most selfless thing you can do, because it ensures that you will be around, truly around, for the long haul.

## The Practice: "Un-Becoming"

The philosopher Socrates famously said, "Know thyself." But for the depleted woman, the more accurate phrase might be **"Un-become thyself."**

You have to "un-become" the version of you that thinks she has to do it all. You have to "un-become" the version of you that is afraid of a messy kitchen. You have to "un-become" the Manager so the Woman can breathe.

This is a practice of subtraction. - Subtract the "shoulds." - Subtract the "performing." - Subtract the "noticing" for people who are perfectly capable of noticing for themselves.

What is left when you subtract all the roles? That is the woman we are looking for. She is the one who will lead you into a life you don't want to escape.

## The Reframe: From Empty to Open

We started this journey by talking about being **depleted**. We talked about feeling empty, like a vessel poured out until there was nothing left but dry cracks.

But as Sarah Miller sat with her lopsided clay bowl, she realized that "empty" wasn't the right word anymore. Through the science of her brain, the naming of her load, the holding of her boundaries, and the design of her systems, she had cleared away the "junk" that was filling her up.

## She wasn't Empty; She was Open

Being depleted means you have nothing left to give. Being open means you finally have the space to receive. You have the space to receive joy, connection, and the version of your life that actually feels like yours.

Sarah looked at her clay bowl and saw a metaphor for her new life. It was a vessel. It wasn't meant to hold a million logistical puzzles. It was meant to hold whatever she chose to put in it. For the first time in ten years, she was the one holding the brush. She was the one choosing the colors.

She had found the calm. She had found herself. But now, she faced the final challenge of the "Recovering Good Girl." How do you make this stay? How do you prevent the "creep" of the chaos from coming back? How do you build a life that is not just a reprieve from burnout, but a permanent architecture of peace?

She had the tools, but she needed the "Long Game." She needed to move from "fixing the crisis" to "designing the future." She realized that the hardest part of the journey wasn't finding the calm—it was believing she was allowed to keep it forever.

She was ready to build a life she didn't want to escape, and she was starting to realize that the most important "system" of all was the one that protected her right to be happy.

# Chapter Ten

# Building a Life You Don't Want to Escape

## The Long Game

In the early spring of 1953, a woman named Beatrice "Bea" Hicks walked into a room of the most powerful engineers in America and waited for someone to tell her she was in the wrong place. Bea was a woman who had spent her life working in rooms where she was the only one. She was an engineer who specialized in gas sensors and environmental controls, which were systems designed to detect invisible threats before they became catastrophes.

On paper, Bea was unlikely to succeed in the "Long Game" of structural change. She was a woman in a field that actively discouraged her presence. She had no massive funding, no traditional "village" of support, and a workload that would have crushed most of her peers. To many, she was an anomaly, a fluke of the system. But Bea understood something about engineering that her male counterparts often missed: you cannot just keep fixing a leaking pipe; you have to redesign the entire pressure system so the leak never happens.

She wasn't interested in "coping" with the friction of being a woman in science. She was interested in **Sustainable Architecture**. She didn't want to survive her career; she wanted to build a profession that she didn't want to escape. Bea went on to found the Society of Women Engineers as a structural buffer rather than a social club. Recognizing that individual "grit" is limited, she emphasized the power of community support, which can be infinite. She stopped trying to be the "exception" and started building the "rule."

## Moving from Coping to Living

Most of the tools we have discussed so far are reactive. We've learned how to calm the nervous system after it's been triggered, how to name the load once it's already heavy, and how to set a boundary when someone is already knocking at the gate. These are essential survival skills. They are the "emergency room" of your mental health.

But you cannot live in the emergency room forever. If the only thing you do is manage the chaos, you are still letting the chaos set the agenda for your life. You are "coping" rather than "living."

Building a life you don't want to escape requires a shift in perspective. It is the move from **Reactive Management** to **Proactive Design**. It is the "Long Game" where you stop asking, *How do I handle this stress?* and start asking, *Why is this stress a recurring part of my daily life, and how do I redesign the situation* to eliminate the source?

## The Values Audit Based on Your Internal Compass

To build a sustainable life, you must first know what you are building *toward*. Most depleted women have lost their internal compass. They make decisions based on "urgency" rather than "importance." They are so busy putting out fires that they haven't noticed they are standing in a forest they never wanted to enter.

This is where we start the **Values Audit**. Think of your calendar as a diary of your values, not just a list of tasks. If we looked at your last seven days, what would they say you value? - If you spent ten hours on work you hate, and zero hours on your health, your calendar says you value your employer's profit over your own heart. - If you spent five hours "performing" domestic perfection and zero hours laughing with your partner, your calendar says you value "the image" over "the connection."

The "Resentment Gap" is the space between what you *say* you value and how you actually spend your time. If you value "Peace" but your life is designed around "Accessibility," you will always feel a constant hum of anger.

To bridge this gap, you must identify your **Non-Negotiable Anchors**. These are the 2-3 things that, if they happen, make the rest of the day feel manageable. For Sarah Miller, her anchors were:

- **The Morning Silence**: 15 minutes of coffee alone before the "Manager" role starts.

- **The Physical Movement**: A 20-minute walk, regardless of the laundry pile.

- **The Unfiltered Connection**: One honest conversation with a friend or Mark where she doesn't have to be "fine."

When these anchors are in place, the rest of the day can be chaotic, but Sarah remains grounded. When she skips them to "be more productive," she loses her center. The Long Game is about protecting these anchors as if your life depends on them, because the *quality* of your life actually does.

# The Three Pillars of a Sustainable Life Architecture

Beatrice Hicks succeeded because she built pillars of support that didn't depend on her daily willpower. You must do the same. A life you don't want to escape is built on three specific structural pillars.

## Pillar 1: The Capacity Buffer

Most women design their lives for their "Best Day" capacity. They assume they will always have 100% energy, perfect health, and zero surprises. Then, a kid gets sick, or a deadline moves, and the entire structure collapses.

The Long Game requires you to design for your **70% Capacity**. This means you deliberately leave white space in your calendar. You say "no" to things even when you technically have the time, to preserve the "buffer." This buffer is what allows you to handle a crisis without falling back into a "Functional Freeze." It is the "safety factor" Bea Hicks would have built into a gas sensor, the extra room that prevents a blowout when the pressure spikes.

## Pillar 2: The Truth Circle

Depletion thrives in isolation. When you feel like the only one who is "failing," you hide. You perform "fine" until you snap.

Building a sustainable life requires at least one relationship where you can be "un-managed." This is someone to whom you can say, "I am drowning today, and I hate everyone in my house," without them trying to "fix" you or judge you. This connection is a pressure-release valve for your nervous system. It reminds you that your worth is not tied to your utility.

## Pillar 3: The Automated Environment

We've discussed the "3 D's," but the Long Game takes this further. It's about creating an environment that "nudges" you toward calm. - It's the "charging station" for your phone that is *outside* your bedroom; it protects your sleep by default. - It's the "uniform" in your closet that eliminates decision fatigue every morning. - It's the "No-Meeting Friday" you negotiate at work to allow your Librarian to catch up on files without the ping of notifications.

## Sarah's "Resentment Gap"

Sarah Miller sat in her car on a Tuesday evening, but she wasn't hiding from her family. She was sitting in the parking lot of a local community center. She had just finished a pottery class, not a 'drop-in' one, but a six-week commitment she had placed on the Family Dashboard.

As she sat there, she looked at her hands, which were still slightly gray from the clay. She thought about the "Values Audit" she had done a month ago. She had realized that her biggest resentment wasn't the chores; it was the fact that she had abandoned her own creativity to become a "Human Sticky Note."

She had found her "Resentment Gap." By filling it with this class, she felt a strange shift in her view of her home. When she walked through the door, she didn't see a list of demands. She saw a place where she lived. Because she had a "territory" that was just hers, she no longer felt like a utility. She felt like a woman who happened to have a family.

Mark met her at the door. "How was the class?"

"It was great," Sarah said, and she meant it. "I'm exhausted, but the good kind of exhausted. Not the 'fried' kind."

Mark nodded. "The kids are in bed. I handled the 'Tuesday Taco' cleanup. You want to sit for a bit?"

Sarah realized that by holding her boundary and doing what she loved, she hadn't made Mark's life harder. She had made their partnership more honest. He wasn't "helping" her; he was maintaining the house so his partner could be a whole human being. The system was no longer a "hack"; it was their new foundation.

## Use the Community as a Buffer for the "Village" Problem

We often hear that "it takes a village," but we live in a world designed to keep us in individual silos. We are expected to manage a modern life using the resources of a single person.

Beatrice Hicks didn't try to change the engineering world alone. She knew that individual voices are easily dismissed, but a "chorus" is impossible to ignore. The Long Game involves building your own "Micro-Village."

This could be a "co-op" for school pickups, a shared meal-prep group, or simply a group text where four women commit to telling the "unfiltered truth" about their week. When you share the mental load with others, you are not being a "burden." You are participating in the ancient human tradition of mutual aid. You are proving that the "Myth of the Natural Caregiver" is a lie. No one is meant to do this alone.

## Handling the Lapse for a Compassionate Reset

The most dangerous moment in the Long Game is the **Lapse**.

You will have a week where the kid gets the flu, the car breaks down, and you snap at your partner. You will have a week where you forget the "Physiological Sigh" and live on coffee and adrenaline.

In the old days, this lapse would lead to a "shame spiral." You would tell yourself, *See? I knew I couldn't be calm. I'm just a high-strung person. This book didn't work.*

But in the Long Game, a lapse is just data. It's a sign that the "pressure" in the system exceeded the current "buffers." You don't need to be better; you need to look at the architecture. - Did I skip my "Non-Negotiable Anchors" this week? - Did I let a "should" creep back onto my plate? - Do I need to re-negotiate a system that isn't working?

Compassion is the "oil" in the machine. Without it, the friction of your own self-judgment will eventually seize the engine. You are a human being, not a gas sensor. You are allowed to be messy. You are allowed to have a bad week. The "Long Game" is about the **Return**, not the **Perfection**.

## A Letter to the Doubter

If you are sitting there thinking, *This sounds great for Sarah, but my life is actually impossible,* I want you to listen closely.

Beatrice Hicks was told her life was impossible, too. She was told she didn't belong in the room. She was told that the systems she wanted to build were unnecessary. She could have spent her life "coping" with the slights and the extra work. Instead, she decided that her energy was too precious to waste on a broken design.

You might feel like you are "stuck" in your depletion. You might feel like your partner will never change, your job will never relent, and your kids will never stop needing you. But you are more powerful than you think. You are in charge of your own internal world.

A calmer "you" is the greatest gift you can give to the people you love. When you are regulated, you are a "Safe Harbor" for your children. When you are joyful, you are a "Spark" for your partner. When you set boundaries, you are a "Model" for your colleagues.

You are not "taking away" from them by choosing yourself. You are ensuring that there is a "you" left to love them.

## The Sustainable Life Blueprint

From here, I want you to define your own blueprint. Don't use mine or Sarah's. Use the data you've gathered from your own nervous system over the last ten chapters.

- **Define Your One Non-Negotiable Anchor**: What is the one thing that must happen for you to feel human? (e.g., 20 minutes of reading, a hot shower, a walk).

- **Identify Your "One Person" of Honesty**: Who is the person you will stop "performing" for?

- **The "Enough" Standard**: What is one area of your life where you will permanently lower the bar to "C-grade" to save your energy?

- **The Pressure Valve**: What is your go-to "Cycle Completer" when the alarm sounds?

Write these down. Place them where you can see them. They are the "blueprints" for the room you are building.

## Write the Future Sentence

Today, I want you to take 1 minute to write 1 sentence about the life you are walking toward.

It shouldn't be a goal like "I will lose ten pounds" or "I will be more productive." It should be a feeling.

- *"I am walking toward a life where I can sit on my porch and feel nothing but the sun on my face."*

- *"I am walking toward a life where a spilled glass of water is just a spilled glass of water."*

- *"I am walking toward a life where I remember my own name."*

Place this sentence where you can see it, on your bathroom mirror, your steering wheel, or your computer monitor. It is your "North Star." Every time you have to set a hard boundary or say "no" to a "should," look at that sentence. Remind yourself that you are not being "difficult"; you are being **Architectural**.

# The Practice of Returning

Sarah Miller stood in her kitchen on a Sunday evening, looking at the same staircase where she had sat with the soccer sock months ago. The house was quiet, but it was a different kind of quiet. It wasn't the "hollow" silence of a woman who was too tired to speak. Instead, it was the "full" silence of a system that was working.

She knew that Monday would bring new challenges. She knew that a plate would eventually drop. But she wasn't afraid of the crash anymore. She had the language for her stress. She had the tools for her body. She had the systems for her home.

She realized that "Calm" was not a destination she had reached. It was a **Practice**. It was something she would have to choose tomorrow morning again, and again on Tuesday afternoon, and again at 2:00 a.m. when the "Good Girl" ghost came to visit.

She wasn't a "Depleted Woman" anymore. She was a woman who knew how to come back to herself.

As we close this chapter and move into the final reflection, I want you to look at the "Long Game" as an invitation rather than a burden. You have the blueprints. You have the tools. The only thing left is to believe that the house you are building is one you truly deserve to live in.

But even with the blueprints in hand, there is one final thing every architect knows: the building is never truly finished. It breathes, it settles, and it requires a constant, gentle "returning" to the original vision. This isn't a failure of the design; it's the beauty of a living thing. And as you prepare to close this book and step back into the "real world," the most important skill you will take with you isn't the ability to stay calm; it's the ability to find your way back when the calm inevitably breaks.

# Conclusion

## The Practice of Returning

**It is 2:14 a.m., and the house is perfectly still.**

Sarah Miller is awake, but for the first time in years, she isn't staring at the ceiling with a heart that feels like a hummingbird trapped in a shoebox. She isn't mentally rehearsing the difficult conversation she needs to have with her boss, nor is she spiraling into a panic because she forgot to buy more dishwasher tabs.

She is awake because she wanted a glass of water. As she stands in her kitchen, bathed in the soft blue glow of the refrigerator light, she notices the laundry basket sitting on the end of the couch. It is overflowing. According to experts Donna Baptiste and Adia Gooden, three months ago, that basket might have felt like a physical weight on her chest, silently judging her and highlighting the pressures and expectations faced by many Black women in their caregiving roles, sometimes making her feel compelled to stay up late folding laundry even when she was exhausted.

Tonight, Sarah looks at the laundry and feels... nothing.

She doesn't feel lazy. She doesn't feel guilty. She recognizes it as a pile of clothes that will be there tomorrow. She takes a slow, deep breath, a Physiological Sigh, by habit now, and feels her ribs expand and her shoulders drop. She is back in her Window of Tolerance. She is no longer the "Human Sticky Note" holding the entire household architecture in her mind. She is just Sarah, a thirsty woman, who is tired in the way people are supposed to be tired at 2:00 a.m., and who is deeply, fundamentally at peace.

According to recent research, women who participate in personal development groups can experience improved mental health and greater resilience, helping them recognize early signs of burnout and take action before exhaustion takes over, guiding them from late-night anxiety to a sense of peace and control over their lives.

## The Pattern of the Return

When we began this journey, the idea of "calm" probably felt like a destination on a map you didn't have the coordinates for. It felt like something that happened to other women, the ones who seemed to have "better" kids, "easier" jobs, or "nicer" partners. You likely felt that your exhaustion was a personal flaw, a leak in your own character that you needed to plug with more discipline and better planners. But remember, progress takes time, and every small step forward is a victory worth celebrating.

But now, you can see the deeper pattern. You can see that your depletion wasn't a "you" problem; it was a system problem.

Everything we have walked through, the spinning plates, the survival mode, the invisible labor, and the perfectionism, is all part of a single, interlocking machine designed to keep you "on" until you burn out. You were a high-functioning person trying to survive a low-functioning environment.

The shift you've made isn't about becoming a "new person." It's about understanding the biology of your own safety. You now know that:

- Calm is a physical state, not a mental choice. You can't think your way out of a stress response; you have to move your way through it.

- The Load is real. Naming the invisible work didn't make the work go away, but it stopped the work from making you feel "crazy." By making the invisible visible, you gave yourself the vocabulary to redistribute the weight.

- Rest is a right, not a reward. You've stopped trying to "earn" your seat at the table of your own life. You've realized that a face mask can't fix a nervous system that is on fire, but a 20-second hug and a "no" can.

- Enough is the new Perfect. You've dismantled the "Good Girl" programming and realized that being "unnecessary" in the kitchen is actually the highest form of success.

These aren't just "tips." They are the building blocks of a new way of living. When Sarah Miller stood in her kitchen and told Leo to talk to Mark about his soccer cleats, she wasn't just delegating a task. She was setting a boundary by saying "no" to unnecessary demands, trusting a system, and protecting her identity all at once. That is where it all connects. That is the moment when the tools stop being things you *do* and become who you *are*.

## The Chorus of Reality

You are not walking this path alone. Remember the "Reddit Chorus" we heard from at the very beginning? Those thousands of voices of women who felt invisible, chronically over-extended, and neurologically "fried"?

When we look back at those voices now, we see they aren't a chorus of failure. They are a chorus of data. They are the proof that the "Myth of the Natural Caregiver" has been a trap for generations. By choosing to step out of that trap, you are participating in a collective "thawing."

Think back to Dr. Aris and her explanation of the "Window of Tolerance." When you first read about it, your window might have felt like a tiny slit, barely wide enough to let in a breath of air. Every small stressor, like the shopping cart bump, the "Wacky Wednesday" socks, or the grainy frosting, was enough to knock you into a rage or a shutdown.

But look at how far you've come. According to Psychology Today, by practicing ways to complete stress cycles and protect your energy, you may notice that your Window of Tolerance has expanded, giving you more capacity to handle everyday challenges." You can handle the chaos of a Tuesday morning without losing the "real you" in the process. You are no longer "glitching" in grocery store parking lots; you are moving through life with a regulated heart.

## The Vision of the Integrated Woman

Mastering this guide doesn't mean your life will be perfect. It doesn't mean your kids will never scream or your boss will never be demanding. It means that when those things happen, they will no longer be able to delete your identity.

Imagine yourself six months from now. You are standing in a room full of people, perhaps at a work holiday party or a family gathering. In the old days, you would have been the "Thermostat," scanning the room to make sure everyone was happy, checking the snack trays, and performing the "Good Girl" role until your scalp ached.

Now, you are just... there. You are laughing at a joke because it's actually funny, not because you're trying to be pleasant. You have a "preference" for the drink you're holding. When someone asks you for a "quick favor" that you don't have the energy for, you use your three-part script without a "guilt hangover." You feel solid. You feel like someone with a "territory" and a "name."

You have built a life you don't want to escape. Your home is no longer a series of logistical puzzles to solve; it is a place where you live. According to a study published in BMC Psychiatry, non-professional caregivers now take on more responsibility for the emotional and practical care of loved ones with depression, often shouldering much of the ongoing monitoring and support that tools like automated systems or family dashboards aim to provide."

## Your Graduation

You started this book as a "Depleted Woman." You were a woman who felt like a ghost in your own life, staring at a half-folded pile of laundry at 2 a.m., caught in a spiral of self-blame. You felt like you were failing at everything because you were trying to do everything.

Today, you are an Integrated Woman.

According to the World Health Organization, burnout results from ongoing workplace stress, and understanding this can empower you to take steps toward your own well-being and peace. You understand that your fatigue isn't a flaw. It's a signal. You have the "Enough Filter" in your pocket and a "Physiological Sigh" in your lungs. According to a review by Arla Day, moving from a mindset of self-sacrifice to one of sustainable presence is an important step in the ongoing process of recovery from burnout, and the journey toward well-being continues beyond this transition. It is the end of your depletion.

## The Final Invitation

As you close this book, you might feel a lingering spark of doubt. The "Good Girl" ghost might whisper that this calm won't last, or that you'll eventually "fail" and return to the chaos.

When that happens, I want you to remember Sarah Miller's clay bowl. It was lopsided, messy, and not "useful." But it was hers. Your life is that bowl. It doesn't have to be perfect to be beautiful. It just has to be yours.

If you have a friend who is currently "hanging by a thread," give her this book. Tell her she isn't failing. Tell her she is just depleted. Tell her there is a way back.

## Your First Act

Tomorrow morning, when your alarm goes off, or when a child's voice wakes you, or when the first "ping" of a notification hits your phone, I want you to do one thing.

Before you get out of bed, before you load the "Manager" files, and before you start the "Labor of Noticing," take three Physiological Sighs. Feel your weight in the bed. Say your own name to yourself.

Then, as you walk into your kitchen, look at the first "plate" that tries to spin your way. Ask yourself: *Is this glass or is it plastic?* If it's plastic, let it drop. Let it bounce. And then, make yourself a cup of coffee and sit in the silence for five minutes. Not because you've earned it, but because you are alive, and that is reason enough.

The life you are walking toward is already here. It's just waiting for you to stop and see it.

Calm is not the absence of the storm; it is the presence of the self within it.

Find her. She's been waiting for you.

Exhale. You're home.

# A Personal Request from the Author

Thank you for reading *Women Too Tired to Keep Pretending.*

If this book helped you feel seen, understood, encouraged, or better equipped to take even one small step toward peace, then I am deeply grateful.

Many women carry invisible burdens every day. Women who are exhausted from holding everything together, saying yes when they want to say no, and pretending they are fine when they are running on empty. More people may benefit from the information in this book, but they may never find it without your help.

If you found this book worthwhile and informative, please consider leaving an honest review. Your words can help another overwhelmed woman recognize the value of this resource and take the first step toward reducing stress, lightening her invisible load, and reclaiming who she was before exhaustion became her normal.

Your review does not have to be long. A few sincere sentences can make a powerful difference.

Thank you for your support, your time, and your willingness to help this message reach the women who need it most.

With appreciation,
George Munson

# Acknowledgements

Writing this book was only possible because I stopped trying to do it all alone. In the spirit of "naming the invisible," I want to acknowledge that while my name is on the cover, a small village of people worked behind the scenes to keep my own "plates" spinning while I sat at my laptop.

**To my daughter,**

Thank you for your patience with me. You are the reason I care so deeply about breaking the cycle of depletion, and your messy, beautiful energy is the heartbeat of this work.

**To Dr. Aris and the researchers whose work fills these pages,**

Thank you for providing the language for our exhaustion. You turned our "mom-guilt" into data and gave us a path back to our nervous systems.

**To my editorial and publishing team,**

Thank you for seeing the value in a book that encourages women to do less. Your belief that "calm" is a worthy pursuit has made all the difference.

**Finally, to the woman reading this,**

Thank you for trusting me with your limited time and energy. You are the reason I wrote this, and I am honored to be in your corner.

# A Note on the Research

If you've made it this far, you know that this book isn't just a collection of "good ideas"; it is built on a foundation of neuroscience, sociology, and behavioral psychology. But because I promised you this wouldn't feel like a textbook, I've tucked the "heavy lifting" back here.

Think of this as the "Why Your Brain is Doing That" cheat sheet. Here is a conversational look at the three pillars of research that inform everything we've discussed.

## Depleted Mother Syndrome (DMS)

While "burnout" is a term we use in the workplace, DMS (often referred to in clinical circles as Parental Burnout) is a specific state of physical, mental, and emotional exhaustion that results from a chronic imbalance between demands and resources.

The research shows that DMS isn't caused by a lack of love for your family; it's caused by the "High Stakes/No Breaks" nature of modern caregiving. When the brain perceives that it is "on call" 24/7 without a predictable endpoint, it stays in a state of hyper-vigilance. Over time, this leads to emotional distancing and a feeling of "failing" at everything. Understanding DMS helps us realize that the "mom-snap" isn't a character flaw; it's a biological "system overload" signal.

## The Stress Response Cycle

Much of our work in Chapters 2 and 5 is based on the groundbreaking research of Drs. Emily and Amelia Nagoski. They identified a crucial distinction: Dealing with your stressors (the laundry, the boss, the crying toddler) is not the same thing as dealing with the stress itself.

Science tells us that stress is a physical tunnel you have to walk through. Even if you finish the task that caused the stress, your body might still be stuck in "fight or flight" mode. This is why you can finally sit down on the couch at 9:00 p.m. but still feel like your heart is racing. To find calm, we don't just need to finish the to-do list; we have to "complete the cycle" using movement, breath, or connection to tell our nervous system, "We are safe now."

## Invisible Labor and the "Mental Load"

In Chapter 3, we talked about the "Human Sticky Note." This is grounded in sociological research regarding Cognitive Labor. Researchers like Allison Daminger have broken this down into four stages: 1. Anticipating a need (realizing the kids will need summer camp weeks before registration opens). 2. Identifying options (researching the camps). 3. Deciding (picking one). 4. Monitoring the outcome (making sure the forms are signed and the gear is packed).

Studies consistently show that even in "equal" households, women often perform the vast majority of the "Anticipating" and "Monitoring" phases. This labor is invisible because it happens in the background of your brain, but it uses the same glucose and neural energy as a high-level board meeting. When we name this labor, we stop wondering why we're tired even when we haven't "done" anything physical yet.

## The Window of Tolerance

The concept of the "Window of Tolerance," developed by Dr. Dan Siegel, is the backbone of our nervous system work. It's the zone where you can handle the ups and downs of life without "flipping your lid" (hyper-arousal) or "shutting down" (hypo-arousal).

Chronic depletion narrows this window. When your window is the size of a postage stamp, a spilled glass of milk feels like a house fire. The goal of the practices in this book isn't to make your life perfect; it's to use neuroplasticity and nervous system regulation to widen that window so you have more room to breathe before you react.

# The Bottom Line

You aren't imagining the weight you're carrying. The science confirms that your brain and body are responding exactly as they were designed to in an impossible environment. You aren't broken; you are a high-functioning system in need of a recalibration.

## Further Reading & Resources

If you found yourself nodding along to Sarah's story or circling the neuroscience sidebars in this book, you are likely ready to look closer at the specific mechanics of reclaiming your life.

The following resources are my personal "gold standard" recommendations, the books and tools that helped me name my own exhaustion and build the frameworks I've shared with you. Think of these as a library of permissions rather than a new to-do list.

### Essential Reading

### On Stress and the Body * ** Burnout:

The Secret to Unlocking the Stress Cycle by Emily Nagoski, PhD, and Amelia Nagoski, DMA If Chapter 2 resonated with you, this is your next step. The Nagoski sisters explain why "completing the cycle" is the key to the difference between chronic depletion and actual relief. It is a fundamental text for any woman living in a state of "on."

## On Boundaries and Mental Space * ** Set Boundaries, Find Peace:

A Guide to Reclaiming Yourself by Nedra Glover Tawwab** Nedra is the reigning queen of the healthy "no." This book provides the specific scripts and psychological courage you need to stop the "guilt hangover" and start protecting your limited energy.

## On Worthiness and Perfectionism * ** The Gifts of Imperfection by Brené Brown:

A classic for a reason. If you struggle with the "Good Girl" programming discussed in Chapter 6, Brené's work on "wholehearted living" and letting go of who you think you're supposed to be is the ultimate antidote to the "never enough" spiral.

## On Invisible Labor and Systems * ** Fair Play: A Game-Changing Solution for When You Have Too Much to Do (and More Life to Live) by Eve Rodsky:

If the "Plate-Spinning" of Chapter 1 felt like a personal attack, Eve Rodsky's system for redistributing domestic labor is the gold standard. It moves the conversation from "helping out" to "full ownership."

## Digital Tools & Communities

- The Nap Ministry (Tricia Hersey): Follow her work on social media or read Rest Is Resistance. Tricia reframes rest as a social justice necessity and a divine right rather than a luxury for the privileged.

- Insight Timer (App): For the "Physiological Sigh" and five-minute nervous system resets. Look for "Yoga Nidra" tracks if you are in a state of deep depletion and need to rest without necessarily sleeping.

- The Motherly Podcast: Specifically, episodes focusing on "Matrescence." Hearing other women articulate the identity shift that comes with motherhood can help you feel less alone in your "identity erosion."

## A Note for the Depleted Reader

Don't buy all of these at once. Pick the one that addresses your deepest ache right now, whether that's your body, your boundaries, or your to-do list—and read it in the "stolen hours" we talked about. You have permission to go slow because your worth is not measured by your productivity, and your recovery is not another chore to finish.

# Quick Guide for "Today's Practices"

## The Daily Practices Found All in One Place

**Your 10-Step Calm Toolkit**

Keep these practices nearby, taped to your fridge, tucked into your planner, or screenshotted on your phone, for those moments when the mental load feels heavy and you need an immediate way to return to yourself.

**Name the Plate**

From Chapter 1: *The Spinning Plates*
Scan your mental to-do list and pick just one "plate" you are currently spinning (e.g., "The Person Who Remembers Spirit Week"). Don't try to drop it yet. Simply say: "I am carrying this right now, and it takes real energy to keep it in the air." Validation is the first step toward relief.

**The Physiological Sigh**

From Chapter 2: *The Science of Survival Mode*
To manually override your "fight or flight" response in under 30 seconds: Take a deep breath in through your nose, followed by a second, shorter

"sip" of air at the very top to fully expand the lungs. Then, let out a very long, slow exhale through your mouth. Repeat three times.

## Make the Invisible, Visible

From Chapter 3: *The Load Nobody Sees*
Choose one piece of invisible labor you performed today, something no one else saw or thanked you for. Say it out loud to yourself, a partner, or a friend: "I spent twenty minutes today coordinating the carpool so tomorrow runs smoothly." Acknowledge it as "real work."

## The Uncancelable Meeting

From Chapter 4: *Why Self-Care Isn't Working*
Look at your calendar for the coming week. Pick a 10-minute block and label it "Restoration." Treat this as an uncancelable meeting with a high-stakes client. During this time, do something from your Restoration Menu, not a chore, not a scroll, just rest.

## Complete a Micro-Cycle

From Chapter 5: *Completing the Stress Cycle*
At the first sign of a "stress signal" (a tight jaw, a short fuse), use a 3-minute cycle completer. Put on one upbeat song and dance, do a "body shake" to release tension, or give someone you love a 20-second hug. Tell your body it is safe now.

## The 70% Defection

From Chapter 6: *The Art of the Enough*
Pick one low-stakes task today and purposely do it at 70% effort. Send the email with a minor typo, leave the laundry in the basket, or serve a "C-grade" dinner. Notice the discomfort that arises, and breathe through it. The world will not collapse.

## The "Unwanted Yes" Script

From Chapter 7: *Saying No Without the Guilt Hangover*
Identify one thing on your plate that you said "yes" to out of obligation. Write down the boundary sentence you wish you had used (e.g., "I'd love to help, but I don't have the capacity this month"). Practice saying it in the mirror to build muscle memory for next time.

## The Full Handoff

From Chapter 8: *Redistributing the Load*
Identify one recurring task and transfer it fully to someone else. This includes the "thinking" and "noticing" parts. If you delegate the grocery shopping, you are no longer responsible for making the list or noticing when the milk is low. Let go of the cognitive overhead.

## The Identity Excavation

From Chapter 9: *Finding Yourself Under All of It*
Think of one hobby or interest you loved before your life became consumed by "the load." Today, tell one person about it: "I used to really love photography," or "I miss playing the piano." Simply naming who you were helps you find who you are.

## Write Your Direction

From Chapter 10: *Building a Life You Don't Want to Escape*
Write down one sentence about the life you are walking toward, one that prioritizes your calm over your performance. (Example: "I am building a life where my peace is more important than my productivity.") Place this note somewhere you will see it every morning.

# Bibliography

If you're the kind of person who sees a list of academic citations and feels your blood pressure rise at the thought of more "homework," take a deep breath. This isn't a peer-review session; it's a map of the giants whose shoulders we're standing on.

The ideas in this book didn't just appear out of thin air. They are rooted in the work of brilliant psychologists, sociologists, and neuroscientists who have dedicated their lives to figuring out why we feel the way we do. If a particular chapter sparked a "lightbulb moment" for you, here is where you can find the deeper story behind the science.

## The Science of "Fry" (The Nervous System)

To understand why Sarah (and all of us) feels like a "human sticky note," I leaned heavily on the Window of Tolerance. This concept was originally coined by Dr. Dan Siegel. It's the foundational idea that we have a "sweet spot" where we can handle life's stressors; when we're depleted, that window shrinks until even a dropped spoon feels like a catastrophe.

## For the "how-to" of calming that system

I look to Dr. Stephen Porges and his Polyvagal Theory. It's a complex body of work, but the "friend-version" is this: your body is constantly scanning for safety, and you can use your breath, specifically that "Physiological Sigh" we practiced, to tell your brain the tiger has left the room.

## The Stress Response Cycle

If Chapter 5 felt like a life raft, you have Emily and Amelia Nagoski to thank. Their groundbreaking book, Burnout: The Secret to Unlocking the Stress Cycle, changed the game for women everywhere. They were the first to articulate that "dealing with the stressor" (the laundry, the boss) is not the same thing as "dealing with the stress" (the physical chemicals in your body). Their research into "completing the cycle" is the backbone of our 3-minute recovery tools.

## Matrescence: The Second Puberty

In Chapter 9, we discussed Matrescence, the total identity shift that happens when you become a mother. This term was first coined by medical anthropologist Dana Raphael in the 1970s and has been beautifully revived by Dr. Aurelie Athan at Columbia University. It's the biological, psychological, and social transition that explains why you don't feel like "the old you." Hint: It's because you aren't, and that's scientifically normal.

## The Invisible Load and Fair Play

The terms "The Labor of Noticing" and "Anticipatory Labor" come from the important work of Eve Rodsky, author of Fair Play, and from the sociological research of Allison Daminger. Daminger's work, specifically on the four stages of mental labor (anticipating, identifying, deciding, and monitoring), helps us realize that "thinking about what's for dinner" is just as much work as cooking it.

## Boundaries and the "Good Girl" Narrative

For the "Guilt Hangover" and the art of the "No," I have been deeply influenced by Nedra Glover Tawwab (Set Boundaries, Find Peace). Her work reminds us that boundaries aren't walls to keep people out; they are gates that keep us from being depleted. Additionally, the "fawn response" (people-pleasing as a survival tactic) is a concept explored by trauma therapist Pete Walker, which helps us view our inability to say "no" with compassion rather than shame.

## Perfectionism and Worthiness

Finally, no guide to calm would be complete without the "Dean of Vulnerability," Dr. Brené Brown. Her decades of research into shame and perfectionism (as in The Gifts of Imperfection) shape our "Art of the Enough." She taught us that "perfectionism is a twenty-ton shield." It's heavy, and it doesn't actually protect us. It just keeps us tired.